*As Barack Obama said, "If y(
along the line gave you sor
teacher somewhere in your l
teachers; this wonderful book means that the wisdom he
so generously shares can reach far and wide for
generations to come. An inspiring read, that gently
reminds us, that we all have the capacity to serve and
the importance of continuously learning.*

**Suki Binning,
Chief Social Worker at Interventions Alliance**

*A treasure of a book full of life-affirming wisdom. A user
manual for self-discovery and personal growth. Ian
makes a compelling case for "servant leadership" and his
commitment to lifelong learning provides a challenge to
us all. A memoir to enjoy and embolden
– highly recommended.*

**Michael Spurr CB,
Chief Executive of HM Prison and Probation Service**

*This book will give you much food for thought and is an
inspiration, an encouragement and an education for
anyone who is pursuing the art of leadership. Especially
leadership that pursues truth, honesty and integrity and
is motivated by genuine humility and curiosity.*

Alan West, Senior Pastor of Luton Christian Fellowship

*Windows and Mirrors' transforms ageless wisdom into
timely insights for all of us who believe
that learning is for life.*

**Matt Bird,
CEO of Relationology**

A reminder of the great adventure of learning, of the opportunities, freedoms and community that curious learning can bring. Written with the humility, compassion and generosity it promotes, this is a uniquely personal and positive story of a life of learning. A great read, not just on learning well, but on living well.

**Dr Gill Attrill OBE,
Deputy Director at HMPPS**

A beautifully written book – authentic, honest and true. Sharing some of Ian's journey has been some of the most fulfilling, and challenging, of my career. To Ian I say directly – keep being curious. It is by far your best, of many, great qualities.

**Amy Franklin,
Director of Operations of
the National Citizen Service Trust**

Ian's wisdom and humility run throughout this wonderful book – a tremendous resource. Windows and Mirrors is helping me to know more about my Lord and myself.

**Renton Baker,
Evangelist**

This book highlights the beauty of truth and love, in leadership. These are not fashionable concepts in the world of business, the holistic wisdom of learning underlines that great leadership requires curiosity and humility. None of us knows as much as all of us.

**Ann-Marie Conway,
Associate Director of Employee
Ownership at Seetec**

Windows and Mirrors
The truths we are coming to know

Copyright © 2024 Ian Porée

The moral rights of the author have been asserted.

Apart from any fair dealing for the purposes of research or private study, or criticism or re-view, as permitted under Copyright, Design and Patents Act 1998, this publication may only be reproduced, stored or transmitted, in any form or by any means, with prior permission in writing of the publishers, or in any case of the reprographic reproduction in accordance with the terms of licences issued by the Copyright Licensing Agency. Enquiries concerning reproduction outside these terms should be sent to the publishers.

Bible quotations are taken from the New International Versions.

PublishU Ltd.

www.PublishU.com

All rights of this publication are reserved.

Thank You

This book exists because of those close to me who encouraged me to share some of my story. The primary driving force was my wife, Tracey, who believed in this project from the start. Thank you for loving me enough to hold the "mirror" of reality in front of me each day, even when it is not the picture I'd like to see. I'm also very grateful for your expert and candid editing skills that have improved this manuscript significantly.

Thank you to my precious children: Mickaela, you will always be my princess, a strong, kind woman filled with wisdom. Josh, you are a caring, courageous and passionate man who stands up for what is right. Know that I love you both so very much. Thank you for sharing your wisdom. To Aaron, my "new son", I love and respect you and am very grateful that you were so willing to join this project and share some of your life lessons.

To Mum (who has already been promoted to glory) and Dad, thank you for loving me and praying for me. To Marc and Mandy, your faithfulness in serving Jesus will always inspire me and our friendship is so precious to me. To Paul and Charles, thank you for looking out for me as older brothers should.

To my spiritual father, Angus, thank you for encouraging me faithfully over many years, including in writing this book. Thank you for your example of simple obedience to Jesus – He gets all the glory for what He has done through us.

To Michael, Radhika, Alan, Gill, Amy, Renton, Suki, Ann-Marie and Matt, and my book writing group, thank you for your wisdom and insight in helping turn my initial manuscript into this much-improved version. Your generosity has been so kind and I am so grateful for our ongoing friendships.

To every person whom I have been fortunate enough to walk alongside, and learn from, I am so grateful for the lessons you have shared to support my life-long journey of learning.

Contents Page

Introduction

Lessons about Learning

    Chapter 1: Lessons about the Posture of Learning

    Chapter 2: Lessons on the Process of Learning

    Chapter 3: Lessons on Sources of Learning

Lessons about Leadership

    Chapter 4: Lessons about Leading Yourself

    Chapter 5: Lessons about Leading Others

    Chapter 6: Lessons about Leading Societal Change

Lessons of Most Importance

    Chapter 7: Lessons on Stewardship and Generosity

    Chapter 8: Lessons on Rest and the Rhythms of Life

    Chapter 9: Lessons on Humility and Gratitude

    Chapter 10: Lessons on Love

Conclusion

About the Author

Sources of Learning

WINDOWS AND MIRRORS

Introduction

Imagine this scene. You are sitting around a large table in the kitchen, after having shared a delicious meal with several generations of your family. One of your grandchildren, in a curious child-like way, then innocently asks you this question, "What are the most important lessons that you have learned in life so far?"

This book in some way is my extended answer to a question like that. It is a collection of the stories of the lessons I have personally gleaned as a life-long learner who embarked on a quest to find truth.

I am a very ordinary person, a rural South African. I have experienced being shaped by discovering truth and applying this truth to guide my life. My story includes my journey of faith, along with many other lessons that I hope are helpful.

The adventure of a life in pursuit of the truth has meant that I have crossed paths with some extraordinary people and I've been to places that I could never have dreamt of.

Here is a small snapshot of some of those experiences: I have visited the huts of traditional Zulu families, as well as met Her Majesty Queen Elizabeth II in her palace. I have been part of the life stories of some poor families in the Philippines, as well as sitting across the table with world-renowned leaders. I have worked on farms and in prisons, as well as in the Houses of Parliament and Number 10 Downing Street. I have volunteered as a youth worker as well as served in the South African Defence Force. I have patented new technology and authored this book. I have been appointed to the Board of impactful charities, private companies and an Executive Agency of the HM Government in the United Kingdom. I have worshipped in rural farm chapels and sat in silence in some of the world's most impressive cathedrals. I have learned about the natural world from barely literate people, whose wisdom has been passed on through generations of living on the land. I have studied in some of the world's leading academic institutions and I have learned lessons from listening to small children.

God only knows what more there is in store for me.

I hope that this book can give a glimpse of the adventures possible if you too choose to follow the path of a curious learner.

In fact, what I have discovered after many decades is that the more that I learn, the more I still have to learn.

As I have given this more thought and discussed this with my children, it has become clear to me that no matter what stage of life we are in, each one of us has lessons we have learnt and are learning. These lessons invite us into the "truths" we are coming to know.

Documenting all the lessons I have learned so far would take too long, and would not make for the most exciting reading, so I thought that I would focus in this book on three main types of lessons: lessons about learning, lessons about leadership (as this topic has dominated my learning in life so far) and lessons on what I have come to know as the most important ones – those of lasting value.

This book intends to offer these lessons as a contribution to your quest for truth. I hope that in some small way, they are helpful to you and that you may take some time to reflect on them.

If they are useful, why not test whether they can in some way be applied to your life and the lives of those around you?

Asking great questions has the power to lead us to new discoveries.

Every one of us is a unique and gifted individual and, because we are unique in the universe, each one of us has immense worth and a contribution to make. We each have coded into our genetics the history of our families and our species.

I have come to learn that the search for truth is an intrinsic part of the human heart. It is in each one of us to be curious if we follow our hearts.

Take each opportunity to learn as a chance to look out the window and see the world around you. Having the curiosity to look beyond where we are, opens up the potential to see and learn new things. If we have the humility to look in the mirror, it will reflect reality, and show things as they are.

One example of 'Windows and Mirrors' from my own experience came when I had the opportunity to serve within Her Majesty's Prison and Probation Service in England and Wales. As I got to know about the people within prisons, I was able to look through the "window" into life within prison. What struck me was that the complex and messy lives of the women and men who live and work within prisons offered a "mirror"; mirror that reflected things about myself. I could see how the pain and suffering, the hopes and dreams and the everyday choices people made reflected things that I too wrestled with. It would be easy to be quick to judge the people in prisons. However, as I looked in the mirror, I had to ask myself, "What would I have done if I had been dealt those cards in life?"

Rather than assuming I was the one who had the answers, I chose to ask questions, listen more and learn from others. The complex world of life in prisons contains much pain, despair and tragedy. However, it also contains beauty, kindness and moments of hope if you are willing to look carefully.

'Windows and Mirrors' will return to these themes and hopefully provide you with your own questions to ask.

I have been married to a strong, courageous and kind wife for over thirty years. I am so grateful to be the father of two adult children and recently a new addition – my much-loved son-in-law. My children have taught me so much and, when I explained to them the idea of writing this book to share my life lessons so far, they agreed to join in the process.

So in addition to some of my lessons, what you will find in each section are the lessons from my twenty-something-year-old children (at the time of writing, Mickaela is twenty-eight, Josh is twenty-six, and Aaron, my son-in-law, is also aged twenty-eight). I am very grateful for their willingness to share their insights. I am once again reminded of how much those of us getting on in years can learn from the next generation.

One of the truths that I have come to know is that none of us know as much as all of us. So let's remember to listen to one another.

The lessons shared in the pages that follow are about the process of having our eyes opened, and how truth has the power to change the way we think. This will change the way we behave and, ultimately, change our hearts. These truths are simply what we have learned so far and we trust that you enjoy reading them.

We are all in danger of losing our child-like genius when we lose our sense of awe.

Chapter 1
Lessons about the Posture of Learning

Are you as teachable as a little child?

The search for truth, like seeking wisdom, is a life-long quest. Like any journey into unknown territory, it requires courage, perseverance and humility.

When I think about the best posture for learning, I think about becoming like a child.

It is from this humble and curious posture, with a sense of wonder and awe, that we should approach learning. The innocence and the openness of a child to explore and encounter new things is how we remain open to the possibility that there is more to this life than we have discovered so far.

There is a hunger, which accompanies curiosity, and staying hungry to learn is how we retain that child-like posture of being "wonder-filled." We are all in danger of losing our child-like genius when we lose our sense of awe.

Gaining wisdom and new insights is at times costly. It is simply true that things of great value come at great cost.

The posture of a humble learner will cost you your ego because you need to lower yourself to be in a position to learn. Perhaps put another way, it is only from a place of knowing our identity that we can embrace humility.

It will require the courage to say, "I don't know." It will also cost you the time and energy it takes to really listen and ponder and think about what you are learning. However, the reward for this humble and curious path makes the price worth paying because it leads to lasting treasure and a satisfying life of adventure.

As with the right posture to learn, it is also true that learning is best done in the community.

The truth is that none of us knows as much as all of us.

I have found that those around me often do my best thinking.

As social creatures, we are designed to learn from one another, to share what we have discovered and to pass on the fragments of our knowledge so that they can be combined with that of others. This creates a richer, deeper and more beautiful picture.

The editing of this book is a great example of learning from and with others. Once I had a rough draft of the manuscript, I shared it with some trusted friends. I am so grateful for their candid feedback. It undoubtedly made this book so much better. Learning works both ways, they shared how some lessons that they had read in the manuscript were helping them reflect on their journey.

If we choose to live only within the boundaries of our current level of knowledge, we are closing the curtains and can't see out the "window." If all your sources of learning come from people just like you, I would encourage you to widen your search and find new voices to listen to, even if their ideas challenge you.

As a practical example, I have in recent years had the opportunity to work with a group of colleagues in an employee-owned business. This meant that in a very real sense, they each had a "say" and a "stake" in how the business was run. What I discovered, time and time again, is that when we took the time to engage a broader group of colleagues in a piece of work, the cumulative wisdom and experience of the group always produced a better outcome.

This included simple examples like getting feedback on a piece of communication being prepared for the business. It also included more complex examples such as refreshing the vision, mission and values of the business. Each time we gathered a diverse group of colleagues from a wide range of roles, especially those colleagues who interacted daily with the participants of our services and listened to their contributions, the outcome was so much better. Admittedly, the process took longer and the path through the decision-making was messier and required a few additional steps. It also required colleagues to be open to changing direction or approach, to be patient to listen, and it required humility and respect for others.

This lesson, like many lessons shared in this book, is best learned through real-life experience.

To get very practical, choose something important to get right. Invite a group of trusted colleagues or friends to help you. Brief them appropriately and allow them to ask clarification questions. I have found it helpful to remind people of your values so that people can hold you accountable for these values. It is also helpful to be clear about the outcome you are seeking. Then, give them time and permission to contribute openly and candidly to the work. Engage the wisdom of others and then really listen to each contribution.

My experience has been that every time I did this with a group of colleagues, the quality of the end product was better. It was better in several ways. There was a greater breadth of wisdom and insight. It was more intimately aligned with the people who would receive the output of the work. It opened my thinking to new aspects that I had not previously considered. Even after I had taken into account the time and additional engagement required, I would say that it was a better overall use of our time.

I can also add that, in addition to the positive contribution to each piece of work, something else happens. Colleagues described how it changed them. They felt included, they had a say, and they could contribute their lessons and also receive learning. This approach strengthened their identity as people who helped others. It also made them feel part of something bigger than themselves.

There is something very human, something wonderful about this kind of co-creation – it does feel special. We all benefit from having a sense of purpose, we all need to feel like we belong and we all benefit from giving of ourselves for the benefit of others.

Why not put co-creation to the test in your own life? I am sure that you will learn something new.

When we discover the truth, the wise thing to do is to listen to it and let it shape us. This is how we grow in understanding. Truth has a purpose and, in the end, if we live by the truth, it will fulfil its purpose in our lives.

I remember being a young boy on the school playground: there were plenty of opportunities to get into a fight. On one occasion I had recently heard about the story told in the Bible that there was a better way than the common "eye for eye" or "tooth for tooth" approach to retaliation. Losing a tooth in a fight would be quite common for a group of boys fighting. The lesson from the story suggested turning the other cheek. After a disagreement over an incident on the playground, one of my classmates grabbed me and hit me, and whilst still screaming at me in anger, he expected me to fight back. That would have been my normal response, having grown up as one of four brothers. I was used to holding my own in a fight.

In this instance, I had been pondering the ancient wisdom of turning the other cheek. I decided to put this truth into practice. I remember standing in front of him, relaxing and simply choosing to smile. I did not respond to the further taunts and verbal abuse. It was very strange to see how this unexpected response was disarming and the boy walked away confused. He also, interestingly, never tried to hit me again. My childlike understanding of this story was limited. The full historical context of this verse about the oppression of the Roman Empire of first-century Jews was a much more complex narrative that I only appreciated over time.

The thing I have learned about "truth" is, that you only really come to know the truth when you are willing to put it to practice.

When we look in the mirror of our lives, we are confronted with reality. It can be tempting to try to change or distort the cold hard facts to try to make things seem better or more palatable than they are. This is especially true if we find our reality uncomfortable.

Ultimately, this turns out to be foolish, as we are then not being shaped by the truth; we are trying to obscure it. We benefit so much more and set a much better example for others if we are willing to humble ourselves, accept the reality of the facts as they are and then seek to make choices shaped by the truth.

In my experience both in life and business, this is a useful test to distinguish between someone willing to learn and grow in wisdom and someone foolish. When you present a person with the facts, with reality, do they accept the truth and think carefully about how they could make changes and learn from the truth? Or do they expend energy and emotion trying to convince you and others that things aren't as they seem and seek to distort reality or deflect attention by blaming others?

Having carried out more performance appraisals of colleagues than I can recall, it is remarkable how these simple principles are consistently true. If you find yourself in a position where you are responsible for assessing someone's performance against their objectives, start by holding up a "mirror" of the facts. You will find that the wise will humbly listen and learn from reality and the foolish typically miss the opportunity to learn by trying to hide or distort the truth.

And now, here are some lessons on the posture of learning from the twenty-something learners:

Over the last few years, we've experienced friends and family starting their own families. As we watch their children develop and begin their learning journey, it has struck me how naturally curious they are. They approach learning with such freedom and delight in discovering new things. We have had long conversations with our niece as she asks "why, why, why" over and over again in her quest for answers.

Having reflected on this, it occurred to me how often I go about my day-to-day life asking so few questions. Children do not feel embarrassed about not having all the answers. Nor do they simply accept what people tell them as truth. They constantly test each new piece of information they are given.

As an adult, I am learning that this is an important lesson to remember. Just following the crowd doesn't necessarily lead you to the truth. Having a curious nature keeps our minds open to the possibility of progress in our daily lives. Challenging our accepted "truths" is ultimately what leads to growth in our friendships, relationships and careers.

I am learning that we need to accept our limitations. Being humble as a learner is essential. I have had to learn to accept that knowing everything there is to know is not an achievable goal; the world around us is too complex. Nevertheless, this should not stop us from striving to learn something small each day because, over a lifetime, we can gain a wealth of knowledge.

I have learned that we need to be prepared to "suck" at something before we master it. I have observed that one of the barriers to learning a new skill – like a new sport, a musical instrument or a new language – is that we are embarrassed at how bad we are at the start. This embarrassment is all about fearing what other people might think or say. The idea that people might make fun of you, for not being good enough, is for many people enough to stop them from trying in the first place. Just when you have built up some confidence in one area of your life, starting over as a beginner, to learn something new, is a fear we must confront.

Often we see children diving straight into something new, without much thought of the possible things that might go wrong. As adults we can be paralysed by fear, unable to take a leap of faith when starting something new. This self-limiting mindset can lead us to believe that we are not very good at many things. We limit our personal and professional development to a "box" in which we are comfortable. In my experience, I have seen senior leaders who are reluctant to learn and integrate new technologies, simply because they are afraid of looking incompetent in front of a more junior colleague. I am trying to learn to find the right balance, to not allow fear to stop me from trying new things.

What I am learning is that if we learn to embrace this initial period of "sucking" and discomfort, these opportunities can become an exciting and rewarding period of learning, and the stories you tell about your mistakes and struggles can be very positive.

It is also usually quite funny. Being able to laugh at yourself is a very healthy test for us all.

A good test of your belief in truth is whether you dare to put it into practice.

Chapter 2
Lessons about the Process of Learning

A good test of your belief in truth is whether you dare to put it into practice.

So far, we have explored the posture of learning, learning from others and how to distinguish the wise learner from the foolish.

We can now turn to the process of learning. I have learned that we often "learn by doing."

The model that comes to mind is that of an apprenticeship. This approach to learning differs from the more purely academic methods. There is of course an important place for theoretical and abstract learning, but, in my experience, this type of studying can only take learning so far.

Knowledge is not of real value until it is applied.

Learning via an apprenticeship involves the very human experience of being with the teacher as they pass on their skills and knowledge. What is so powerful about this ancient model of learning, like a master carpenter teaching their apprentice to work with wood, is that, as humans, we place greater value on what we see done, than on advice or instructions we hear. You will no doubt be familiar with the age-old saying: "Children do what you do; not what you say." I believe this is true.

In an apprenticeship, the student observes the teacher at work. They get to see another person acting and interacting in the role that they aspire to. Wise students will take the time to listen to the instructions of the teacher. They will observe and ask questions. This will help them learn the skills and gain insights into why things are done in that way. This first phase of an apprenticeship journey is like looking through the "window." It is a door that our teacher can open for us. This learning is through a process of modelling behaviour and actions. Then, in a safe space with appropriate boundaries, allow the student to try things themselves and be rewarded and corrected.

I remember as a child learning to improve my skills in a particular sport, like cricket, squash or volleyball. The coach would take the time to repeatedly show us how the shot was played. After seeing and hearing the right way to play the shot, we would try to replicate it over and over with hours of practice.

My dad was a good squash player, and as his four boys grew older and stronger, fitter and faster, his skill and technique were still more than a match for us, long after we could outrun or outlast him physically. It was not only his teaching about how to hold the racket, or how to adjust power and direction, but he also taught us through his example how to move and how to anticipate what your opponent did. We always suspected that he held back a few tricks to keep us humble and as a father myself, I can see why that might be a good idea now that my children are fitter and stronger than me.

Using an example from the natural world (which I will do regularly throughout this book), there appears to be something intriguing about how more complex organisms, like mammals, learn.

For example, the way an adult orca trains her offspring is a real-life apprenticeship, and the stakes are very high as this is the process by which that individual will survive and thrive, or not. Perhaps we are designed with the ability to pass on lessons from one generation to another. The truth is that there is very little that is new under the sun and we can learn from biological systems, which have evolved over millennia.

To look forward to the future, we often need to look even further back in history to find the truth.

As biological research techniques continue to advance, we are learning lessons, which are nothing short of mind-blowing (for example, the fact that plants communicate). We are learning that one generation of plants can actually pass on vital information to the next generation and nurture them through "adolescence" into maturity. The next time you are in a natural forest, perhaps take the time to pause. Imagine how the main "matriarchal tree" is a teacher. It is surrounded by "apprentices" learning through interconnected root systems and sharing important information necessary for survival.

A wise apprentice needs to take the time to think. When we put our ordered thoughts into action we reinforce the lessons we are learning.

This moves the "knowing" from our heads to our hearts, hands and feet. When we know something in our hearts and our bodies, it is a lesson that has been tested and proven in the real world. We can be tempted to give greater weight to rational decisions made with our heads, but heart-led decisions are fully authentic. A full knowledge requires accessing the full range of our senses.

The goal of an apprenticeship, however, is not simply to learn the necessary knowledge. It is of course to progress to being competent in doing the work. The teacher will allow the student to apply the learning so far. If the students apply themselves, they can progress to doing things on their own but still benefit from the "mirror" of reality provided by the teacher.

This holistic teaching approach allows for a two-way exchange. In a very human way, one person passes on wisdom and knowledge to another, giving the student a precious gift. It also, in my experience, gives the teacher a meaningful reward. This reward is not straightforward to explain, but something powerful happens to our identity when we realise that we are the kind of person who can help others.

In my opinion, the most powerful part of the apprenticeship journey comes when the cycle is repeated, and the mature students are ready to take on apprentices of their own. This self-replicating cycle is how we, as a species, have passed on wisdom for thousands of years.

Why not find someone you can follow and become someone worth following?

True science is a quest for truth. With advanced technology that allows us to study the human brain, we are getting a better understanding of how we think and learn.

I had the opportunity to be trained as a research scientist. This approach, the scientific method, to adding new information to the cumulative knowledge of humanity requires first studying to understand what is currently known in a particular field. It requires then posing questions about what is not yet known.

This is one of those truths that I have come to know. If we are willing to pay attention to the boundaries of our ignorance and the limits of our knowledge, we can find new insights.

This requires courage to intentionally go beyond what we comfortably think we know and ask a few extra questions. This is easier to do when things are not working when things go wrong. However, I have also observed that if we don't understand why something is working well, we are not well prepared for when things stop working.

I started work as an applied scientist. I was doing chemical and industrial technology research and, later in life, also did social science research in the field of applied criminology. Whether it was patenting new industrial chemical processes, or exploring new insights into human behaviour change, I came to learn that applied science has parallels with apprenticeships. As a scientist, you must humbly learn from those who have come before you, and then you try to contribute. You get to pass on new insight to the next curious learners.

If done properly, and with integrity, science requires very high standards of ethics. If you do not treat your scientific findings ethically and humbly, you will not discover the real truth. It will take you down the wrong path. You have to hold yourself to the standard, which insists, "I will not falsify the data." This principle works in life as well. As soon as you are tempted to spread or record "un-truth", then you are not adding things of value to the world but rather undermining value. Your falsified results could cause others to be led astray, sometimes at great cost.

In some real sense, the quest for truth is an apprenticeship of learning in which you subjugate yourself to an ethic of truth.

Telling the truth is not just necessary for science, it is the right thing to do even if it is inconvenient or unpopular. Our modern society seems to be too willing to falsify information, which then leads people astray. The truth is not always what we want to hear, but that does not change the fact that it is true.

A good test of your belief in truth is whether you dare to put it into practice.

As you discover the truth and put it into action, you form a solid foundation upon which to build your life. If your life is built on proven and unshakable truth then, when the inevitable storms of life come, your life will not fall apart. It will stand firm. The opposite is also true. If you have built your life on a set of vague or untrue ideas that you have made up yourself, when life gets hard, your foundation will shift or crack and so will your life.

We cannot avoid struggles in life; they are part of life on earth. However, we can make wise choices about the truths we build our lives on.

Truth is all around us and is there for the finding; however, it is a mystery unfolding rather than a one-off problem to be solved.

As a scientist, I have had to learn that whilst we may want to have each bit of evidence neatly fit our model or hypothesis for how things work, things are not that simple. We have to be willing to stay open to the unfolding mystery and to stay humble knowing that we all have so much more to learn. To discover the truth we often need a new level of thinking, but we should always remember that we are to keep tender hearts.

I have experienced working with some of the world's experts in the field of criminology and applied criminology, and they taught me so much about the process of learning. These kind and very smart colleagues are relentless in their pursuit of new insight. They are courageous enough to immerse themselves in some of the most challenging fields of human behaviour to help broken, damaged and often dangerous individuals. These individuals can hold their own in the most prestigious academic settings but choose to work at the frontline of public services (like prisons), so that they can apply their insight to changing lives.

I am so grateful to have had the pleasure of studying under some brilliant academics. One in particular, Professor Alison Liebling, modelled what it means to pursue truth in the most powerfully positive and academically rigorous way, in the toughest of human environments. She applied the practice of "appreciative inquiry" to studying the quality of life of women and men in prison.

Appreciative inquiry is a method of study and problem-solving which focuses on the strengths and positive aspects of people's lives, and complex systems, rather than only focusing on weaknesses and more visible failures. In a very human way, Alison and her team shed fresh insight into the complex and often traumatic world of prisons. They did this by being willing to learn from the strengths of people's lives and their best experiences. By being up close and personal with the real people in prison, by showing up with respect, compassion and humility, and meticulously applying very high academic standards to the work, they were able to shed light on the dark and often misunderstood world of prisons.

I am so grateful to have seen firsthand how this positive approach gave the people involved fresh hope. I would recommend using "appreciative inquiry" if you are ever faced leading complex human change. I am confident that this positive, "strengths-based" and "hope-filled" approach will shed new light and provide a positive way forward.

We have covered the posture of a learner, and we have explored the process of learning, so now it is worth giving some thought to the context in which we learn.

There is a lesson that I have learned about learning, which is counter-cultural to our modern, western society. It is that discomfort, pain and suffering are not distractions to a life of learning, but rather they are necessary paths to deeper understanding.

When we prematurely seek comfort and quickly try to get relief from pain, we are in danger of missing the opportunity to learn lessons. If we choose to run from or deny our pain, if we are not willing to sit with the reality of our pain, then we might miss an important lesson, or store up in our mind and our bodies unprocessed hurt.

If our immediate goal is to manage or mitigate the pain, to cope for some time, then denial may meet this short-term objective. Simply surviving trauma does take real courage. What if our goal is actually to come to a place of peace? What if we want to grow in our relationships to find deeper union and to transform into the person we want to become? Then only facing the truth – not denial – will achieve this goal.

I have learned to ask myself the question, "What lessons do I still need to learn from this painful situation?"

It is an intentional choice not to move on too quickly from a difficult and painful set of circumstances until I can ponder the lessons to be learned. We live in a culture that drives us to do what feels good. We have a distraction for every kind of discomfort and a pill to dull any pain.

My conclusion is that some of my most important life lessons have come from my most painful seasons.

There is something significant about being in the desert, in a barren place, stripped of comforts and distractions. Adversity and hardship focus our minds in a way that reminds me of how valuable failure is for learning. The way that I have experienced learning during times of hardship or failure, is that I seem to be more willing to ask difficult questions to myself. To look in the mirror and see things as they are.

Facing reality seems to shine a light on aspects of my character, my motives, my behaviour and my choices. Despite being uncomfortable, and at times devastating, reality enables me to see things more clearly. So, when I am in the midst of a challenging season, I have learned to use the "mirror" of reality to ask what lessons we could learn. The pain might just be the device that our brain uses to mark this event as an important lesson. If we pull away from the pain too quickly, it might rob us of the lesson.

It is also true that in good times, it is more difficult for us to face reality. In my conversations with trusted friends and mentors, we have often observed that success is much more dangerous for the condition of our soul than failure is. It could be that our greatest challenge is not dealing with failure; it is how we cope with the weight of success. This is a heavy load and both our lives and our character need a strong foundation to endure. When things seem to be only good, it is easy to stop paying attention to the small things. We stop asking the hard questions, we take shortcuts and make assumptions.

I remember a time when I was still a student and I had just completed a year where my academic achievements were, objectively, exceptional. I had achieved extremely high grades in all subjects and this set me up for a future filled with possibilities. The problem was that I took these results for granted. I spent the next year enjoying life to the full and the disciplined work required to achieve those standards lapsed. Unsurprisingly, my results also suffered and came very close to undermining my plans for further study. I had to have an embarrassing conversation with a professor who could not make sense of my poor results. It was humbling and I went from being the top of the class to having to take additional classes to get back on track. In hindsight, I am very grateful for the lessons that I learned at this time because they served me well in the years ahead. I was able to return to the high standards I set myself. The difference was that I had become a more humble and disciplined learner.

A more humble and curious approach to learning is to be relentless in understanding why things are working. We will return to these lessons when exploring leading ourselves, but the truth is that success is not the highest ideal against which we should measure who we are becoming.

Being faithful is more important than being successful.

We need to learn how to treat both triumph and disaster in the same way. Events do not determine how we feel, what matters is how we interpret the events.

And now for some more lessons on the process of learning from the twenty-something learners:

One of the most formative periods of our childhood is the formal schooling system. This often shapes our attitudes and relationship with learning early on in life. Having completed almost twenty years of formal education through school, sixth form and university, I have spent time reflecting on the benefits and pitfalls of our current traditional education systems.

These formal settings do provide us with a clear structure, pre-determined goals and a group of peers to learn alongside. However, I have come to understand that this approach to education often misses the mark in providing us with some of life's most important lessons. In my experience, formal schooling focuses on simply delivering and being able to reproduce a sub-set of preselected knowledge. Although this has value, I believe education should equip children to think deeper than this, search for their questions and encourage curiosity and life-long learning.

For many years this led me to attribute the value of learning something to achieving a pre-determined amount of knowledge on a subject or to pass exams. Ultimately this led to a feeling of dissatisfaction in the learning process and a lack of motivation to continue after each goal had been achieved.

Having chosen a career where life-long learning is crucial to my development and success, my relationship with learning had to change. Rather than viewing learning as something to pass an exam or finish another year of schooling, I've had to learn to engage in the process of continual learning. This builds on the foundations I already have and is not simply ticking a box. By trying to find ways to enjoy the journey, rather than simply reach a destination, I have found far more satisfaction as a learner.

Although the periods I have spent reading and studying for exams have given me important "book-based" knowledge, things in real life, more often than not, aren't as simple as they are in a textbook. Over the early years of my career, the real-life experiences, or time spent carefully thinking about and reflecting on a challenging situation or my human relationships, have often brought me far more understanding about myself and the world around me than any exam I've written. These real-life situations, often messy and sometimes painful, give us the opportunities to apply the knowledge we've gained in formal teaching settings. Although we will not always get these things right, without applying what we think we know, we cannot truly grow.

What real-life learning brings is the opportunity to learn from and with others, sharing the complexity of life, not pretending to have all the answers, but humbly sharing life and learning together.

In the process of adapting my approach to learning, I have learned that I need to be patient with myself. I am learning that the art of learning is itself a skill; a skill that you can learn and improve over time. This lesson is something that I am still working on. The shift in focus from more short-term, tick-box achievements to more lifelong learning goals has been challenging.

I am going to try to keep practising the art of learning.

Growing up, I watched my dad devote time each day to learning and growth, not for a deadline or an enforced goal, and I am slowly learning the value of this discipline.

To be able to learn something new, we must be open to exposing ourselves to new ideas and methods so that our skills or knowledge continue to broaden and deepen over time. This requires discipline and persistence even when progress is slow. I have often found that just when you think that you have all the answers, life provides you with a new challenge or setback requiring a new level of learning.

If you want to master a new skill or take your learning to a deeper level, then you simply cannot do this in a hurry. It requires discipline and persistence, and learning the lesson of persistence might be one of the most important skills to master. I have come to realise that the more you know, the more you realise that there is so much more to learn.

IAN PORÉE

If you are looking for a more interesting life; don't try to be interesting. Be more interested in interesting people.

Chapter 3
Lessons on Sources of Learning

If you seek truth with all your heart, you will find it.

A curious learner needs the right posture; we need a proven learning process and we should be willing to learn in whatever context we find ourselves. We should also consider the sources of our learning.

There are two valuable sources that I have drawn from in my quest for truth.

The first source for me has been learning from the natural world. We have so much to learn from all of creation. There is a kind of truth found in our biology; it is coded within our DNA. Taking the time to observe, listen to and think about how the natural world works, has not only given me so much joy, but it is also where I often turn to for inspiration.

Studying the work of the greatest designers gives us ideas and inspiration. There is simply nothing made by human beings that compares to the wonder, beauty, complexity and sheer "awesomeness" of the natural universe.

When I am struggling with a complex business problem, I try to take time to observe natural systems. I have often concluded that the most elegant designs in nature provide clues to help find solutions to challenges in our modern world.

We have invented so many advanced technologies, but we still have so much to learn from the things we human beings did not create.

From the smallest creatures to immense global systems, there seems to be an almost infinite number of ways in which we can grow in knowledge by observing the master craftsmanship of the world around us. One way to think about this is that when we spend time in an environment, which contains nothing made by humans, then we can only consider things of divine origin.

I would also encourage you to simply take the time to observe the natural world, without an agenda – just with curiosity. Simply remain present and alert.

I find such joy just quietly and intentionally looking at the small details of the creatures all around us, or gazing at the clouds or the stars, or sitting by the ocean. The sounds and smells and constant movement of the sea are a source of tranquillity to me. In a very real way, it restores my soul to sit beside the sea. The vastness of the ocean reminds me that I am only a tiny part of an awesome universe.

Here is an example of how I have learned from the natural world. When I have pondered how to live a healthy, sustainable and contented life, I think about a tree. The tree is rooted in the soil which provides the support to hold it firmly in place. It draws life-sustaining nutrients and moisture from the soil and its roots are interconnected with the other plants around it.

When a tree is "ill", the first thing an arborist will check is the soil surrounding the tree. More often than not, the clue to the ill health of the plant is found in nutrient deficiencies in the soil. If I am unwell, physically or mentally, it helps to check the "soil" around my life for deficiencies or unhealthy habits.

The plant must also encounter the sun, the wind and the rain, which help it to grow strong. It is interesting to me that when we grow trees under artificial conditions, with ideal light, water and nutrients, but no wind, the tree grows quickly but it is weak and cannot hold up the weight of its branches. The constant buffering of the wind, while it is growing, is necessary to build strength in the trunk of the tree.

I too need to recognise that the discomfort, the struggle that comes from doing hard things, is making me stronger and more resilient. When a previously hard thing becomes comfortable or easy, then it is no longer building my strength.

I have had the opportunity to study at multiple academic institutions, covering a wide range of subjects and having read extensively. I have also worked in many different industries, in many different countries and cultures, and a wide range of sectors including the private, public and charitable sectors. I am so grateful to have learned from so many passionate, smart, capable and kind colleagues. All of these relationships and environments have been rich sources of learning.

I would encourage you to make the most of the opportunities that life and work present to you to learn from those around you, even from or especially from, those who are not like you.

If you are looking for a more interesting life; don't try to be interesting. Be more interested in interesting people.

I will now turn to the second and perhaps most important source of learning in my search for truth. This is the one source that has been the consistent reference point for my life for the past forty-plus years. I have read it daily and tried to learn the lessons contained within it and tried to put these lessons into practice. I have done this with mixed success. In my weakness and human limitations, I have not always been the best apprentice. However, I know that this source contains a depth of wisdom and truth that is more real to me today than it has ever been.

This source is very ancient, a truly unique collection of ancient writing preserved through thousands of years of human history in a way that is nothing short of remarkable. The authors describe the text as having divine inspiration, as being instructions to orient our lives towards finding the way, to finding life and to finding the truth. I have found all of this to be true and have sought to make the truth revealed in this ancient text the foundation upon which I am building my life.

In an uncertain world, in the information age, I have come to learn that this source of ancient wisdom can still provide us with a solid rock upon which we can stand. The source that I am describing is the Bible.

Learning starts with thinking. If we spend time thinking deeply about the truth, like that recorded in these ancient texts, we give our minds a reference point, the way a builder would use a plumb line to ensure that each brick in the wall is in line and level. When we build on truth we get a much better perspective on how things should be, or could be better, rather than just how they are. There is a better way to live than the patterns offered to us by our modern world and culture.

Left to my thinking, I would have chosen a life seeking my selfish pleasures rather than learning the lesson that true joy comes from serving others.

I have come to know that being a curious learner is a wise path and that each decision we make determines in some way both the direction and the quality of our lives.

To make wise decisions we need to take the time to learn what the wise thing to do is. I think that this starts with getting a clear perspective of reality by knowing the truth.

The twenty-something learners have their perspective:

When reflecting on the sources of my learning over the years, I have realised the most important places that I've gained knowledge and understanding were actually from people themselves. Seeking advice and constructive feedback from those with more experience and knowledge than myself has been my most valuable source of new insight and personal development. Although doing this can lead to criticism, by actively seeking feedback you give yourself a valuable gift as a learner. If you choose wisely, people can bring you both comfort in difficult times and challenge you when you may need it.

There are certain things I firmly believe to be true that I would not be able to give a scientific reason or explanation as to why. I believe that throughout human history and through to this present day, we have been able to use God as a source of explaining such things.

For example, in the Old Testament, there are several commands or rules given relating to prohibiting unclean foods or other types of contamination. This was thousands of years before humans had any idea of bacteria or microbiology and yet they were able to discover that if they did not follow certain rules then bad things would happen. They explained these choices as coming from a Higher Power.

If we look at more modern examples, recently I've noticed trends across a variety of fields. Take for example the idea of "gratitude diaries" in fields such as cognitive behavioural therapy to help people who may be suffering from mental health disorders such as anxiety or depression. Several therapists are also using techniques where they get clients to visualise good things happening to people close to them, people that they care about, as a way to improve their mood and mental well-being. In addition to this, there has also been an exponential growth in mindset or performance coaches who teach "visualisation" techniques to individuals, especially in professional sports, as a powerful way of achieving enhanced performance and realisation of goals.

Modern neuroscience and the invention of brain scanning technology have made it possible to provide scientific evidence that supports the real-life benefits of these techniques. However, for thousands of years, people have been performing these actions as part of religious practices. For example, the practices and rituals associated with meditation and prayer have taught people to put into practice this advice for years: advice like saying "sorry" for the things they have done wrong, intentionally being grateful for the things that they have and praying selflessly for what they would like to happen for other people and themselves.

It is so tempting in our comfortable, modern world to choose the easy road. When I reflect on how life on earth has changed so rapidly over the last few hundred years alone, I can't help but wonder if life has become too simple for us complex beings. As a result, I have intentionally started to choose the "harder path" in day-to-day life. By introducing "challenges" such as cold showers, fasting and high-intensity workouts into my daily routine, especially when I don't feel like doing them, I am trying to build resilience for when the inevitable unexpected challenges of life do come my way. By purposefully teaching myself in this way that I can do difficult things when they do arise in unforeseen circumstances, I will already have this knowledge and experience to rely on. I do believe that we won't find new insights of lasting value unless we are willing to pay the price of learning to take the difficult path to learn those lessons.

It may seem a strange lesson to add to a chapter on learning, but I couldn't help but include a few thoughts on the important lesson of "un-learning" things. Most of what we learn comes from the people and experiences we have of the world around us. A habit is simply a learnt behaviour and it is common for each of us to learn bad habits. We learn through seeing a poor example from someone else, or through ignorance and even 'untruth'. It could simply be a habit formed by doing what was most convenient or in an attempt to avoid discomfort.

For example, in modern-day life, many of us can comfortably sit and scroll through social media on the phone for hours. The companies that design these apps use powerful nudges and prompts to keep us engaged. However, the truth is, which is backed up by scientific research, that it is detrimental to our mental health and well-being. So why do we still do it? When we face the truth about bad habits, the challenge becomes how do we "unlearn" what has become part of our lives? This is something I am still learning.

Whatever the cause of adopting bad habits, being willing to hear the truth and looking in the mirror at our actions allows us to change.

This is a choice. If we dare to face reality, and we discipline ourselves to form new habits, we can change for the better.

IAN PORÉE

The choice we all face is between trying to make an impression versus a life of trying to make a difference.

Chapter 4
Lessons about Leading Yourself

Who are you becoming?

I have come to learn that to lead yourself well, you need to take the time to know yourself.

To know yourself requires an ongoing exploration of asking questions about your purpose, what and who matters, and how you can find a place where you belong.

So let me share a brief background about myself.

I am the third of four sons. I was raised in rural South Africa in a loving family. Not perfect of course; we have our share of dysfunction. As brothers, we lived full and active outdoor lives spending much of our time either on the sports field, in the swimming pool or the ocean. In a sports-crazy culture, we loved our sport and competed hard. For me that included putting in many hours in the swimming pool and competing nationally.

I learned many important lessons through competitive sport, including how to discipline yourself to train hard and that without perseverance you will not reach your full potential. To succeed in high-level competitive sport you must be willing to push yourself beyond your limits. If you are unwilling to push past the pain and discomfort then you will simply not achieve higher levels of performance.

I can clearly remember a good example of this lesson. My swimming coach would make us swim as fast as we could and then she'd say, "When you get to the flags, close to the finish, go faster." She was preparing us for that moment in the race when the difference between winning or not was decided. This took hours of exhausting training to be ready for the decisive moment in the race.

Like so many situations in life, it takes training and the right mindset to finish strong.

I learned at an early age that we all have choices in life. The path to excellence is difficult and requires daily discipline and perseverance. There were many days when it would have been more comfortable to stay in bed, or "hang out" with my friends rather than get back in the pool. I am grateful to have learned the lessons about self-disciple at this age, but I should also issue a note of caution. If you build your identity on your achievements and your performance, there is a risk that you will focus more on what you can get done, rather than pay attention to who you are becoming.

It is simply not true that the success we achieve determines our value.

The truth is that our value is found in who we are, Whose we are and who we are becoming.

Continuing my childhood story, one aspect that took me until my early adulthood to better understand, and required the help of a skilled professional, was my deep need for acceptance.

Sadly, for many of us, a toxic script from our childhood can make its way into our hearts.

For me, it was that I never quite believed that I mattered.

What was the point of me? This led me to strive for approval from those around me. I fell into the pattern of "performing" to earn acceptance, to show that I could be of use. I became highly driven to exceed people's expectations and as a result, I often over-achieved. Through much pain and heartache, I have come to learn that a life-long quest to earn the approval of others is simply like chasing after the wind.

The truth is that if you have not found meaning in life, no amount of success will give you true meaning and purpose.

If it is the outcome you are pursuing, like fame, influence or wealth, then eventually even if you achieve these things they will often be empty, or even crush you. These things should be the outcomes of life pursuing something of lasting value, like becoming the kind of person who grows in wisdom and serves others. If you then experience fame and prosperity, they are less likely to define you or destroy you.

Success only magnifies what is already within you, the good and the bad.

It would be better to measure your success in terms of how much you can give to others, rather than how much you can get from others.

I have learned that pursuing success is a poor foundation upon which to build a life, especially if you aim to develop the strength of character necessary to stand firm through life's inevitable trials and struggles.

Ultimately, it is a lie to believe that we are not acceptable.

It is a lie to try to live your life for the acceptance of others. Each one of us, including me, is precious and has eternal value. The truth about us is that we are dearly loved.

I am very grateful to have been born with a set of natural talents. These, combined with my early need for approval and an inbuilt "South African style competitiveness", drove me to sporting and academic success. I discovered early on in life that I had the gift of leadership. This is not something that I can take credit for in any way, which is why I call it a "gift." The adults around me observed from as early as my primary school years that I had the aptitude to take responsibility for a group or team, and that others would follow. They consistently selected me for team or school leadership roles. I was not the most talented member of the teams I led, but I did enjoy trying to inspire each person to fulfil their potential in pursuit of the team's goals.

This pattern has continued throughout my life so far. I learned as early as my teenage years, that we are all given different gifts or talents and it is incumbent on each one of us to discover what talents we have and then take time to steward and develop those talents.

It was also during my teenage years that I was confronted with what turned out to be a life-changing choice.

Up until that point, I was pursuing selfish pleasure and adventure. With the benefit of hindsight, these were very self-centred choices and I am very grateful for both the intervention of caring adults and a divine encounter, which caused me to have a hard look in the mirror. What I saw was not pretty, and it was not a good trajectory for me or those around me. I could see two distinct paths ahead of me. One continued to focus on myself and my success and pleasure, and the other was a more humble path, one which would lead to a life of service.

The choice we all face is between trying to make an impression versus a life of trying to make a difference.

Through some close family friends, I had a divine encounter. As a teenager, I experienced an invitation from the Son of God, Jesus Christ. He posed an important question. Did I believe that He is who He says He is? He said He is God. He was there at the very beginning of time. He said He is the light of the world. He is the ultimate source of truth. He invited me to follow Him. I became His apprentice. I chose to put Him at the centre of my world and everything since has been a little clearer. I have been learning His ways ever since.

Many decades later I can confirm that He is now my closest and most precious Friend. He has proven to be faithful in every way. No one has cared for me like He has. He has stood by me through my most painful times. I know He loves me with all His heart; He delights in me. I am learning to love Him the same, with all my heart.

Despite being God in human form, Jesus came to serve and not be served. He is the ultimate example of servant leadership. Sadly, due to our human frailties, I have had to learn that when following His example we often need to separate Jesus from what people have done in Jesus' name.

As a young man, I invested considerable time and effort

in studying leadership. I have been doing this ever since and, forty-plus years later, I am still a student of leadership, seeking to learn and grow as a leader.

I would like to share three types of lessons that I have learned on leadership. They are lessons on leading yourself, lessons on leading others and lessons on leading societal change.

Everyone can lead, and leadership matters. It is important to remember, however, that as a leader you cannot rise above the limitations of your character, no matter how talented you are.

Who we are becoming is so much more important than what we are doing.

If we measure our sense of self-worth by what we can get done, we are stuck on a hamster wheel that will never quite satisfy us. I have come to learn that a more secure foundation upon which to build your identity is to first understand the truth about who you are and then focus on the person you are becoming.

For example, if you believe, as I do, that being someone who is kind is one of the most important things we can aspire to, then taking the time and energy to become a person that others experience as kind, is a higher priority than great achievements.

Now, I should add a warning to this lesson. When you choose to focus on who you are becoming ahead of what you have achieved, you are choosing a path that says that your character comes ahead of your comfort. This means that you will need to make short-term choices which will feel uncomfortable, perhaps painful or even unfair at times. These choices will cause you to say "no" to your desire for instant gratification.

"Becoming" is a slow process and it is a difficult and narrow road.

It can also be a lonely road as it is not what our modern society presents as the obvious or the best way. Our consumer-centric society would rather "you do you" or "do what feels good" – without limits. However, as the Bible reminds us, it is possible to gain the whole world but still lose our souls.

A curious person might ask, "How do you decide who you want to become?"

This is of course something each one of us needs to carefully consider. In my experience, this is where drawing on the ancient wisdom of the Bible, starting with wisdom that originates from a truly Divine Source, is worth exploring. I have been on this path for many decades. I remain a "work in progress"; just ask those closest to me. However, I am starting to see more clearly what is of most importance.

I have chosen to put love as my highest and most important aim.

As someone ambitious about what can be achieved and is not afraid of challenges, I have also had to learn important self-leadership lessons about how to change. When learning how to lead yourself, one of the things that is necessary is how you become the person that you aspire to be.

This discipline of self-efficacy is a necessary life lesson. It is the ability to establish the patterns, habits and behaviours that will enable you to become the person you aim to be.

I have had to learn this lesson the hard way. I am a very determined person; I know how to strive for a goal or a target. These are skills I learned at an early age in competitive sports. Setting targets and measuring performance to know the reality of how fast you are, provides tools to focus your efforts. However, I think that because I was so accustomed to trying to gain approval and acceptance, I thought that it was by sheer willpower and determination that we achieved our goals in life.

The truth is, that some short-term goals and apparent progress can be made in this way. However, if you want to achieve real and lasting progress, you need to put in the work to "train" and not just "try" harder.

This is one of the important lessons that I have learned about leading yourself – focus on "training" and not just on "trying" hard.

Become the kind of person who trains regularly in any area of life where you have set yourself goals. As any experienced trainer will teach you, you need to break down your training into smaller, achievable goals. Steady, deliberate progress will beat a short-term peak of extreme effort, followed by the inevitable trough of despair and disillusionment.

This training also requires that we stay open to new ideas and have the humility to stay open to learning from others and the courage to try new things. This is how we adapt and improve over time. Remember that we all need to start with initial goals. These need to be achievable and we need to be patient. Then, if you keep at it, you will notice real progress over months and years. If someone offers you a quick fix, an easy hack to short-circuit the training and achieve amazing results, my advice is to politely decline. There is no credible way to bypass the hard work of making changes that last.

This analogy works well for exercise, or if you are trying to lose weight or learn a new skill. You can't, apart from a few exceptional individuals, run a marathon if you have not put in the training. This also applies to our character, so remember that the saying "practice makes perfect" is not the whole story.

It is possible to practise a bad habit well. If, for example, you decide that it is important for your character development to be a person of integrity, then you need to train yourself through small daily acts to live as a person of integrity. This is not easy.

Real integrity is tested when you think no one will know what you have done. We may escape human knowledge of our actions, but the truth is that there is a divine record of our life story, which includes every detail.

So to become a person of integrity, or someone who tells the truth, will require that you practise telling the truth. If you practise telling the truth in little things, even when it is uncomfortable or exposes your frailties and weaknesses, then when the stakes are much higher, when the consequences for speaking the truth could have a lasting impact, you would have better prepared yourself for that situation.

Being prepared requires daily training.

Let me use a small example if I was not charged for an item at the supermarket. I could choose to simply ignore it because no one is likely to find out, or I could blame the supermarket staff, or I could rationalise that they are a large enough organisation so it will not matter. Or I could choose to act with integrity. I could go back and pay for the item.

Another trivial example might be if I tried to throw my food wrapper into the bin and it misses and falls to the floor. I could walk away, assuming it is not a big deal and that someone else will clean it up. Or, a person of integrity would acknowledge the mistake, respect others, walk back to pick it up and put it in the right place.

I have chosen trivial examples to emphasise the point that we build character through thousands of very small acts. I believe that we should live in a manner that assumes that someone is always watching.

Here is a weightier example of "who" we are becoming in our relationships. Perhaps you have decided to become the kind of person who forgives others. Being forgiving is an essential component of demonstrating love; it requires the posture of humility because we are acknowledging that we too need forgiveness.

To become a person who consistently forgives requires that we train each day to quickly forgive those around us when they get things wrong. This also, of course, applies to learning to forgive ourselves.

Forgiveness is not so much about choosing to forget the

wrong or the harm caused. It is the opposite because it requires accurate remembering. The thing that happened was wrong, it hurt and it matters. However, forgiveness is the power to choose to give up being in control of who will be the ultimate judge. When we forgive quickly, we are choosing not to carry the weight of the offence and never allow it to take root in us as that can lead to bitterness. The weight of bitterness is too heavy for any relationship to carry. It is of course also important to pay attention to how our behaviour and choices impact those around us. If we practise forgiving ourselves for hurting or doing wrong to others, we must also take the time to get to the root of why we treat someone we love in that way.

If you regularly practise forgiving small things, you become a person who forgives. Then, even when you encounter much more painful and serious matters, your heart is already oriented to forgive.

We all need forgiveness and, in the end, will be forgiven in line with the way we forgive others.

For the avoidance of doubt, there are of course situations where we need to separate the issue of forgiveness from protection from further harm. Holding people to account and putting clear boundaries in place to prevent future harm is necessary and is not the same as the choice to forgive, especially for seriously harmful acts. The reality is that forgiveness does not mean that there are no consequences; there almost always are. Real justice is still required.

Leading ourselves towards who we aim to become is a choice of character over comfort.

It requires that we take practical steps to create new habits, and then train ourselves to embed those habits into our daily or weekly schedules.

A helpful lesson that I have learned in this regard is to decide in advance what these choices and priorities will be.

Once you have decided, allocate the time for training and building new habits. Put this time in your schedule or calendar as a commitment that you have made in advance. There is something that happens to our ability to follow through on a plan to change something in ourselves that is much more likely to happen if it is written down as an appointment in the calendar.

Here are some personal examples of practices that I have implemented which continue to help me to become the person I aspire to be.

I chose many years ago to try to become the kind of person who lives according to all that is good, beautiful and true. I have found that this requires daily orientation or re-orientation towards this aim. I need daily practices which start first thing each morning. I search the Bible to re-align my heart and my mind towards what is true. My practice is to get up early to set aside time in silence and solitude. I take time to read, time to meditate and time to talk to God in prayer.

One way I like to describe this daily devotional practice is to imagine what it would be like to start each day with the smell of freshly baked bread in your home. It takes time and discipline to bake bread each day, but there is nothing quite like the smell of it. If we try to get away with bread that is a few days old or only buy someone else's bread, it just isn't the same and it quickly gets stale. "Fresh bread" each morning is the essence of this daily time I spend talking to my Heavenly Father.

The pursuit of truth takes time; it cannot be achieved in a hurry or on the run.

As I discussed in the lessons about learning, there are two sources of wisdom and truth upon which I have built and continue to build my life. The first is reading the ancient collection of the books of the Bible. The other is "reading", through observation, the "books of the natural world." I speak to the Source behind the ancient writings of the Bible about what I have read, and about what I observe in the natural world.

This for me is a way to practise remembering what is true.

Praying is just about having a conversation with God. It is primarily about our relationship. For most people of faith, simple prayers are the most common. We tend to pray, "help", when we are in trouble, "why", when we are confused and "thanks" when we are grateful. Prayer is a way of starting each day by being grateful, a way of remembering the Source of truth and our deeper purpose. It is a safe place to talk about everyday life and lessons for each day. When we look in the "mirror" of our lives, we see the flaws and the pain, we name it for what it is and then we are ready to ask for help. This is a way to align my heart and mind with what is good, beautiful and true before being exposed to the world around me. It has been a daily practice that has served to anchor my life for many decades.

Prayer is the opposite of training my neural networks through anxious thoughts. I have learned that it is not useful to constantly worry, either about day-to-day things like "What's my next meal" or "What should I wear today" or bigger things, like important life decisions. Once again we can learn from the natural world. The birds can find food without producing any of it and the natural flowers are so beautiful without worrying about how they look.

Each day has enough trouble of its own; we do not need to worry about tomorrow.

I have come to learn that what we think about first thing each day, and last thing each day before we go to sleep, have the most impact on forming the neural pathways in our brains which shape our thinking. If you "meditate" on anxious thoughts or fears, especially when these thoughts have their source in untrue things said about you, then your brain is reinforcing these pathways the more time you process these thoughts. In contrast, if you think about things that are good and kind and true, you are becoming a more hopeful person.

Our emotions are not very good guides to what is right and true because they are much more inclined to direct us towards convenience and comfort.

This path requires building habits that support you being able to realign your choices towards something of real value, rather than simply responding to your immediate desires. I have learned that comfort and seeking pleasure is not always good for me, but that it is very easy to follow this path in the small choices we make each day.

The truth is that nothing of significance can be achieved

without discomfort.

One practice, which is gaining popularity as a counter-cultural way of resisting the consumer culture of our modern world, is to commit to a life of simplicity or minimalism. Choosing to live a simple and modest life, can avoid some of the traps of consumerism and reduce our impact on the planet. The wisdom in this approach is that we avoid the weight of too many possessions. They create the illusion of bringing happiness and joy, but often the enjoyment is fleeting and we are left with the clutter of more things in life to weigh us down. It seems counter-intuitive, but subtraction, taking things away, can often be more helpful than adding or multiplying what we have.

If we keep life simple and fully appreciate what is around us, and who is around us, we can find joy.

Another related and ancient practice of subtraction, or abstaining from, is the practice of fasting. Fasting is when you do not eat any food or drink other than water (or black coffee in my case). Fasting from social media or your favourite TV series is not what I mean by fasting, although that is a kind of intentional abstinence that I am sure can be very beneficial in our modern online and over-distracted world.

Fasting is a very direct way of training your body to not be enslaved by your immediate physical desires. This practice requires training – not simply trying (I have found that my willpower is not very effective against the body's response to withholding food). I have learned from personal experience that when you intentionally withhold food and only drink water for twelve, twenty-four or thirty-six hours, your need to remove the discomfort of hunger surfaces with a very loud and persuasive set of arguments. These "arguments" often entice you to satisfy your hunger with something comforting or pleasurable like a sugary treat or some delicious carbohydrates. The reality is that you should expect to start small, like for example skipping one meal. Also, expect to fail often, but don't quit; simply learn from your training and get back on track. I constantly need to ask for Divine grace to follow this path.

I have a friend who has a very clever, simple tactic during fasting. She simply acknowledges the hunger when it surfaces and says, "Hello hunger, I hear you, but we will not be eating until later." This helps to put the urge to eat into its rightful place, which should be below our higher-order priorities as we learn that our purpose and meaning are derived from much more than the food we eat.

So many of us in the Western world have become accustomed to satisfying our physical desires almost instantly, and the array of food we can access at a whim is staggering. This mindset overflows into all areas of our lives.

A good life – a fulfilled life – is more than delicious bread/our favourite food alone. Training your body and your mind to withhold pleasure, in this case, food, allows us to search for a source of life and truth in deeper things.

I also aspire to become a person of generosity.

If you want to become a person who is content with what you have and is grateful for the good things in your life, then you can learn the lessons about how to become a person who cheerfully gives to others. This kind of person's security or identity does not depend on how much "stuff" they have. The systems and ideas which have been embraced in Western culture would have us believe that we need more "stuff" to be happy; that there is only a limited amount of resources so we should get as much as we can, and that accumulating wealth will make us feel secure and happy.

This is simply not true. I believe that it is better to give than to receive.

If I want to become a generous person, then I need to train myself by performing regular acts of generosity. To become the kind of person who is generous, you could decide in advance what percentage of your income you will give away before you even receive it. By sharing the first portion of what you earn, you are acknowledging the true Source of your income. You are learning to live within the boundaries of what is left. Your generosity in sharing with others is also, of course, making the world a better and kinder place.

In my personal experience over many decades, whilst this financial principle may not make immediate sense to an accountant, if you apply this ancient wisdom from the Bible, then you too will discover that rather than having less over time, this generosity multiplies in more ways than just your wealth.

Your life is richer when you become a person of generosity.

Underpinning my learning about self-leadership and intentionally choosing to live my life by prioritising who I am becoming rather than what I am doing or achieving, is the truth that each one of us has intrinsic worth. We are unique and masterfully created beings and it is worth remembering that about yourself, as well as those around you.

I have learned that when you assign worth to yourself and others, then it becomes clearer why we should treat both ourselves and others with dignity and respect. If we get to know who we are, and who created us, then we can better order our choices about why we are here on earth and what contribution we can make to the planet and the lives of those around us.

Accepting the weakness, frailty and brokenness of our own lives, and knowing the truth about ourselves, changes how we see both ourselves and others.

As I have already said, I am a rural South African from modest beginnings; nobody special. However, once I encountered the truth about who I am, and Whose I am, then I could see how this nobody could be of service to somebody and play a small part in making the world a bit better than how I found it.

Here's what the twenty-something learners have to say about self-leadership lessons:

I believe all leadership begins with self-leadership. Self-leadership requires an investment in yourself, taking time to understand what is important to you and what values you want to form the foundation of your choices or behaviours.

We are all unique individuals with different strengths and

weaknesses, likes and dislikes, but to lead ourselves well, we need to know what "truths" we are building our lives on.

This requires us to be transparent with ourselves and to accept our flaws and imperfections. Acknowledging these things means we are better placed to set ourselves meaningful goals towards self-development.

For example, for me, kindness is very high on my list of values. This is a choice that I can make, as I lead myself, which is not dependent on the behaviour of others. I have learned that in leading myself, at times, I need to extend compassion and kindness towards myself. This is a way of accepting my limitations and faults. Kindness is not a weakness; it is simply being clear and real.

Another thing I have learnt about self-leadership is the importance of accountability. In life, our actions are the only real example of something we have complete control over. I am learning to reflect on both good and bad experiences in life by focusing my attention on the things within my control, rather than spending time and energy worrying about the things outside of my control. I have found both acceptance and peace of mind in dealing with things I cannot control, as well as clarity on what I can personally learn from these experiences.

To use a very simple example to explain this point, if you are out for a walk you might get caught in the rain. Instead of complaining about being unlucky, you can ask yourself the question, what could I have done differently to be better prepared? Of course, you could have checked the weather forecast or taken an umbrella. Although this is a very simple example, it illustrates the point of how adjusting your focus in this way provides room for growth and learning.

Further to this, I am learning that whilst we are not in control of many circumstances in life, we can choose how we perceive life. If I simply reframe what is ahead of me as something "I get to do", rather than "something I have to do", I have found that this changes my whole perspective.

This mindset gives me a sense of purpose and it results in me being grateful for the opportunities ahead of me, which motivates and energises me to take on the task or challenge. When I have completed that task, I can also reflect on the opportunity of getting to do it, which leaves me more open to learning from it.

Good self-leadership indeed takes a lot of self-discipline. When no one is watching, or holding you accountable for achieving your goals, self-discipline can easily fall by the wayside. I have found that I often need some form of accountability to keep on track with achieving my goals. I find it useful to write down my goals and to set in advance the expected timelines to achieve a goal. It also helps to tell someone else about them, like a trusted friend, a family member or partner.

Part of this lesson is also the importance of keeping your word to yourself. If you tell yourself you are going to do something – whether it's to get more sleep, exercise more, or complete a project on time – you should do what you said you would. This builds trust and respect for yourself, which turns out to be important for leading yourself in the right way. You become a person who does what they say they will do.

I believe that this ability to build trust in ourselves will serve us well in life as we seek to serve others well.

> ***The truth is that we need people to respect us, not like us.***

Chapter 5
Lesson about Leading Others

It will be different with you; you will serve and not be served.

Each one of us is likely, at some point in our lives, to be asked to lead others. I am grateful to have led others and the most important lesson that I have learned, once again gleaned from the ancient wisdom of the Bible, is that leadership, like love, is about serving others.

We find true meaning in life when we give ourselves to a cause – something greater than ourselves. In a very practical sense, when you are willing to wash someone's feet, you get a much better understanding of why they walk as they do.

We explored in the previous chapter, that leading starts with knowing yourself. I have come to learn that you cannot lead others effectively until you have reached a place in life where you do not need their approval for your sense of identity and purpose. Simply put, if you are not leading yourself well, you will not be able to lead others well.

Here is the golden rule about life, and leadership: Ask yourself in a given situation, what would you want other people to do for you, and how would you like them to treat you? Then, grab the initiative, and do it for them.

See people as having intrinsic and lasting value; that is how we all want to be seen.

Learn to disagree with people without needing to be disagreeable or needing to demonise them. Always have faith in people, believing that we all have the potential to be good. Learn to listen to people without interrupting and always keep control of your tongue. Be the first to say that you are sorry.

We all want to be treated with kindness and respect, and not be pre-judged or misunderstood.

Be kind and courageous enough to speak the truth.

There is a common perception that leadership is a hierarchy, which sets the leader at the top and that the game is to climb the ladder to eventually achieve the top spot. Whilst this may seem like the right order of things, there is a better way.

By choosing the posture of a servant and by serving people where they are, by actually caring for and loving people, by putting what is best for them first, it turns out that this is the most important leadership lesson of all.

I have had the opportunity to lead for over forty years. As a curious learner, I have had the opportunity to observe, listen to and learn from a very diverse range of leaders and leadership styles.

The most inspirational leaders that I have followed have modelled servant-hearted leadership. I have seen leaders in action in the most stressful and challenging circumstances. Situations which have included life-threatening choices or decisions impacting the lives of hundreds of thousands of people.

Selfless leaders always stand out ahead of self-centred or

self-important leaders.

A truly servant-hearted leader is inspirational and earns both respect and extraordinary loyalty. I have found this to be the best example to try to follow. It is undoubtedly the harder path to take. I am so grateful to have known real people who lead like this, and so have been able to look through the "window" of their lives. I have come to learn that servant leadership is one of the best safeguards to those who lead, and to those who follow.

I wrote these words a few years back to try to express what I have learned from one such leader. Due to being a public figure, I have decided not to include their name. I would encourage you to read these words as the reflection that I saw in the "mirror" of this leader's life daily:

> "A tribute to authentic servant leadership: After decades of committed, high-quality public service, the time has come for this leader to hand over the baton. Times of transition like this are inevitably disruptive, but I wanted to take a moment to reflect on my personal experience of what I describe as an excellent example of 'servant leadership.'
>
> I have had the unique opportunity to work alongside this leader for almost fifteen years. I have learned so much from him and could expand on so many aspects of his character, such as his kindness, his resilience, his patience, his candour and his impressive self-control under pressure. Somehow, amid some very difficult circumstances, he was able to find time to care for others caught

up in the latest 'storm.' He cared for each individual, regardless of his or her status in life. For the avoidance of doubt, I also acknowledge that he is not perfect; he has weaknesses, faults, frustrations and frailties like the rest of us. There are, however, three things about him that I would like to personally highlight, as they have made a lasting impact on me:

Integrity – There are volumes written on leadership about integrity, and I have had the opportunity to work with leaders in government, business, the social sector and faith-based organisations. It remains rare in my experience to find people whose actions consistently, over many years, align with their words. Many leaders aspire to lead with integrity, but I have found this leader not just wanting to be seen to do the right thing but to be a man of integrity. It is who he is. Amid very challenging circumstances, he has consistently sought to speak the truth, even at his own cost, and to the best of his ability he has tried to do what is right. Inevitably, in challenging roles like this, there is considerable criticism. This can easily cause one to be defensive, but he has sought to focus on speaking the truth candidly rather than simply reacting to those who seek to blame. It takes incredible strength to listen and learn rather than mount an immediate defence. There have been times when it would have been easier or convenient to allow the finger of blame to be pointed at others, but that is not how he operates. He took responsibility. He led. I have seen him carefully take the time to learn from difficult events, listen and remain respectful throughout. He also made the tough calls and dealt decisively with critical issues. Yet, he somehow always retained his humanity and treated people with dignity.

I have been personally inspired to try to always treat other people the way I would want to be treated – following his example.

Selfless public service – At the very heart of being a public servant is the important truth that we are here to serve others; to serve the public. It has however been my experience that even committed public servants find it hard to lead without keeping one eye on their ambitions. This leader is one of the very best examples I have come across of someone who has consistently put the mission and purpose ahead of himself, ahead of his reputation. He is one of the most selfless leaders I know. As anyone in leadership knows, there is a high personal price to pay to lead with authenticity and he and his family have given up so much for his enduring public service.

He took his responsibilities seriously and with diligence, and he commanded tremendous respect. Yet it always felt to me like I was working with him, not for him.

Courage in the arena – The past decade has included some good times, but mainly challenging times for public service. However, he has always put himself in the arena, at the front of the battle, leading by example. There are many commentators who at times like this speak their minds about the problems, and I'm sure that we can learn something from them. However, I have learned to pay careful attention to those whose voices come from being in the arena, and who have dared to stand firm. His courage, perseverance and resilience mark him out as a man of substance and I am so grateful to have learned so much from him. His commitment and compassion mean that whatever he does he will continue to change lives.

With humility, I am so grateful to call this selfless, authentic, courageous leader, my friend."

Leaders teach us most by their example.

The next lesson on leading others that I want to share has been a lot harder for me to put into practice. I explained earlier in this book that I was predisposed as a child to try hard to earn people's approval. This led me at times as a leader to be tempted to say what I thought people wanted to hear in order to gain their acceptance.

It is not difficult to work out what someone would like to hear. However, this is a slippery slope. It ends up including the information that is likely to be well received, and downplaying or omitting to include the information which is likely to be challenging. Reality is often uncomfortable. I have caused hurt to colleagues who would have been better served if I dared to speak the whole truth.

As soon as you find yourself carefully presenting the best version of events, you are obscuring the true picture. Whilst in the short term this might feel better, I have come to learn the hard way that clarity is kindness and it is essential for trust. Often, the kindest thing that you can do for someone is to tell them the truth.

I have had the benefit of living with someone, my wife, for over three decades who is relentless in telling me the truth. This is seldom comfortable but I have learned that the people I trust the most are the ones who are willing to risk offending me or putting our relationship at risk, to tell me the truth.

At pivotal moments in my life, I have had people who love me enough to tell me the truth. I can recall a time when I needed to make a big decision about the direction my career would take. I had a plan and talked it through with someone I trusted, a father figure and a mentor. He simply held up a "mirror" by telling me the truth. He agreed that my plans were good plans that would serve a small group of people. He then challenged me to ask why it was that I did not have the faith to believe in attempting something much greater, something beyond what I could achieve on my own, and something that would cost me so much more. I would have to put my trust in Someone much greater than myself.

He asked if I was willing to pay the price to choose a path of service with a much bigger vision. He did not tell me what to decide. He painted a clearer picture of reality. I am so grateful that someone loved me enough to speak the truth at a time when I might have taken an easier path. I chose the path of service.

Perhaps you could be the person who speaks the truth to someone you love, to help them see more clearly.

To lead well, we need to get comfortable with being uncomfortable. The saying, "iron sharpens iron", is a good way to think about hearing the truth. There might need to be "sparks" to sharpen our focus. Those who care for us are willing to risk discomfort for our good.

I have learned that even when you think that you have all the answers, create the conditions for your colleagues, or trusted friends, to tell you what they think. A good discipline to learn is that if you don't know the next step, then ask. Everyone can play the part of a truth-teller if we create a safe space. Listen to what people say. You may not agree with them but show them the respect to let them be heard.

It has been my experience that there is almost always wisdom to be found in these uncomfortable conversations. The truth is more likely to emerge. Yes, this takes more time and requires emotional resilience, but it brings things into the light and servant-hearted leaders should expect to be held to this level of accountability.

Several times over my working career I have needed to restructure a team or large parts of the organisation. There is nothing easy or comfortable about telling someone that they no longer have a job. This is especially difficult when it has nothing to do with their performance or contribution. Sadly, I have seen too many examples of senior leaders who are quick to delegate these hard conversations to others or blame others for the difficult choices. My advice is that when difficult conversations are required, leaders should be more visible than ever. Personally listening to the painful human stories of the impact of these decisions, facing the inevitable anger and frustration and of course, the tears, is the minimum requirement for leaders. It is in these times that I have learned so much.

If you want to be there to take credit for the success of your team, then you should be even more willing to be present at the most difficult times.

Another way of expressing this lesson is to simply be the kind of person who says, "yes" or "no." If you are clear by saying what you mean, and do what you said you would do, then you will see trust grow with the people in your life. It sounds too simple. Try it and you will see that it is not easy.

It is hard to get leverage over someone willing to walk away and stand by their "no." Make the hard choice and stay true to yourself. I have found that this, over time, ends up being a better way.

Become the kind of person who, if you say you will do something, then people can count on it being done. Leaders who do what they say build trust. There is of course an important implication for this approach to leading others, which is, be careful what you commit to. Think before you speak. Take the time to count the cost in terms of time, energy, resources and the impact on others before making commitments. Be willing to say "no."

The truth is that the same person who you are trying so

hard not to displease by saying "no," is most likely the very person who will eventually be disappointed because you said "yes."

The truth is that we need people to respect us, not like us.

This is another lesson a mentor has instilled in me. Learning to say "no" is one of the clues to gaining respect. Never underestimate the impact on those around you when you dare to say "no." It is also true that it is fairly easy for people to tell the difference between someone who says "no" and means it, so much so that you know that it would be a waste of your time to ask again, and someone whose "no" simply means "maybe" and if you ask again you might get a different answer.

If you have the opportunity to lead others, then nothing can be more important than to articulate a vision for the future.

Without vision, people lose their way.

Leaders need to look out the "window" to see where we should go in the future. Our direction is more important than our speed. People won't follow a leader who has no vision. Why should people leave "here" to go "there"?

It is the responsibility of the leader to ensure that people understand and embrace the vision. If people do not know where you are going, then you as the leader haven't made it clear. It is your job. Take a good hard look in the mirror. Work out how to make the vision simple and clear. Make it convincing and compelling. Embed it in everything you do and, of course, live it out each day.

One of the best examples that I have personally been part of, in casting vision, was during my time on the Board of the Agency which was responsible for the Prison and Probation Service in England and Wales. At a time of considerable organisational change, we were tasked with bringing together into one organisation prisons and probation. The culture of these two organisations was fundamentally different, even though the people serving in each organisation shared very strong vocational values of public service. The inevitable tensions between public protection, supporting the victims of crime and supporting individuals through their rehabilitation journey were very apparent. Using an inclusive approach of co-creation with colleagues across the breadth of the Agency, we created a new mission statement, 'Preventing Victims by Changing Lives.' This simple but powerful vision gave all colleagues the language to see how their particular roles contributed. Our talented head of communications led an amazing campaign called 'Changing Lives' which had colleagues from every part of the Agency, in their own words, expressing how they came to work each day and were "changing lives." The wave of positive engagement, during one of the most challenging periods of the organisation's history, was a testament to the power of a clear vision. Another good test of vision is that it stands the test of time, and this mission statement remains in place fifteen years later.

As important as a vision is, never forget that people and relationships come before vision. We are not meant to lead on our own. We do not achieve great things on our own. Leadership, like life, is not a solo sport. Invest time and energy in building trusted relationships with the people on your team and those who lead you.

If you try to lead alone, and if you do not learn to share the load of leadership, you will find that you will get worn out and get off track. We are designed for the community; to be interdependent. The earlier lesson that "none of us is as smart as all of us" applies very much to leading others. Leaders need the humility of learning from all those around them and understanding that trust is something that is earned.

I have learned that what makes the posture of a servant-hearted leader so powerful, is that it starts with a genuine interest in each person you serve. We build our deepest relationships with those who know us and are for us.

Yet again we can glean lessons from the natural world. Leading people and having leadership responsibility for organisations for any length of time will bring you to the point where you need to consider issues like growth, change, productivity and organisational effectiveness. Like plants, we as individuals, teams and whole organisations, need to face times of pruning to enable optimum performance. I share these lessons because I have personal experience of applying these principles in the real world and seeing the depths of wisdom contained within them. I not only discovered these lessons from reading the Bible, but as I was raised on a farm, I got to learn these lessons by practising them each season on the farm.

The most straightforward step in pruning is to remove the branches of a plant that have stopped producing anything useful, typically called "deadwood." You will find the equivalent in large organisations. Whilst the colleagues are showing up and doing what they have always done, in reality, they often know that their function is no longer contributing.

As a word of caution, sadly, I have seen the term "deadwood" used pejoratively about people, which is very unkind and extremely demoralising. People should always be treated with dignity and respect.

Removing these branches is ultimately the best thing for the person as well as for the organisation. The benefit of removing these branches is that it opens up space for new growth, to shape the plant according to the future vision rather than being tied to structures of the past. It also allows natural light to reach all the parts of the plant or the organisation that need deep transparency and new energy. A clear picture of reality is necessary to optimise organisational performance. Until you clear away unproductive legacy structures it is often more difficult to see clearly. Sometimes the sheer weight of these unnecessary structures and overheads drain the organisation of its strength

The next step in pruning is to find the branches that are unhealthy and show little or no sign of recovery. Removing these "sick" branches allows the plant, or the organisation, to focus all their resources on the growth and productivity required for future health. This pruning removes the unproductive use of resources or excessive drains on reserves and investment capital. In my experience, organisations typically take too long to acknowledge the branch that is sick, irrecoverable and is best removed. Leaders can often be at fault, especially if that project or initiative is something that the leader is personally invested in. This is one of those moments when we need to look hard at the facts and face reality.

The final type of branches which need pruning are good branches but not necessarily great branches. These are healthy in their own right, but they are not aligned with the future vision of the organisation. I have found these to be the toughest decisions. However, these are the kinds of disciplined decisions that great organisations make to elevate their performance to be sustainable over time. Building a great organisation should not be based on your immediate circumstances, but rather it depends on disciplined decision-making and staying true to your purpose over decades.

As with pruning plants, these actions, when leading organisations, allow all the remaining branches to receive the full benefit of the nutrients and sufficient light and energy to thrive. The overall shape of the plant is now fully aligned with the mission and purpose, even if it appears smaller. This is how to position your organisation to deliver the highest yield in the economic or market conditions you find yourself in.

The way that I have come to think about this lesson is that disciplined action and course correction serves the purpose of re-aligning each season with reality.

The truth is that pruning is painful. We should not pretend it is not. It impacts the lives of real people in our organisations. It must therefore always be done carefully and respectfully, but this pain is for a purpose. This lesson is something that we can all apply to our own lives and our organisations. If we do this wisely, with wise counsel, we will be able to measure the outcome in more "fruit" and better long-term outcomes.

There is a special category of leading others that I think is important to include. This is leading at home. This may be the most important opportunity in life to demonstrate servant leadership.

I am so grateful to have been a husband to my wife for over thirty years, and a father to my daughter and my son and, more recently, my son-in-law. The truth is that leaders need to lead at home with greater intensity and commitment than they lead at work. I will always be so grateful that just a few months after my daughter was born, my wife confronted me with an important question. This was one of those "look in the mirror moments." She asked whether I was going to show up and be present as a dad, to be hands-on in the day-to-day lives of my children. She reminded me that we had been united in our decision to try to have children. Having received the precious gift of a child, I was confronted by a choice to either follow what was culturally normal at the time, to mainly focus on my job and my career, or to be present for my children. The sober reality check allowed me to re-prioritise and commit to engaging in the lives of my children. They are now both adults and I can say, that alongside my wife, these are the most important and meaningful relationships in my life. This might not have been the case if I had not been confronted by the truth.

Training our children to become curious learners, to seek the truth themselves and to learn to lead themselves, might be one of the most important things we get to do on earth.

I have no greater joy than to hear and see my children walking their journey of seeking the truth.

I made a covenant commitment to my wife to love and serve her. It is not a contractual arrangement based on her upholding her side of the agreement. It is a promise I made before God to love her, by serving her, no matter what circumstances came our way.

This partnership, as equal partners, despite being uniquely different people, has been the basis of our shared approach to serving our family. We have very different personalities, but we have continued to learn from each other through the inevitable conflict. We have worked hard to try to stay united on important matters regarding the children. We have of course had our share of pain and frustration and, but for the grace of God, our marriage may not have survived on several occasions. It is humbling to remember all how I have fallen short as a husband and a father. The truth is that regardless of my good intentions, my actions have often simply been selfish and foolish. I am very grateful that my wife has often dared to hold up a "mirror" for me to face reality.

After decades of serving in leadership positions I have come to know that like the posture of learning requires humility, so does leadership. We all have weaknesses and we all carry a level of brokenness in our lives. We also can encourage and inspire or discourage and cause disillusion. The truth is that hurt people hurt people, damaged people damage people, forgiven people forgive people and those who have received mercy can offer mercy.

Good leaders lead by example. So, be quick to admit your mistakes and ask for forgiveness. This says something important about your basic integrity as a leader.

When you see behaviour that is misaligned with the values and culture of your organisation, it is better to explain rather than excuse poor behaviour. Don't ignore it. A clear explanation creates the opportunity to shed light on something, to see it from all sides and to accept what is true. An excuse from the leader, or a colleague, only seeks to hide or run from the truth. It is an attempt to cover up what is true.

It is our role as leaders to create an environment in which our colleagues feel safe.

I have learned that the signs indicating that people feel safe include a willingness to speak up and to disagree with the direction of travel or the thinking in the room. Another important sign, which is important to look out for, and to model as a leader, is the willingness to ask for help.

Transparency and clarity are essential ingredients of trust, and without trust, our relationships only ever operate at a surface level. This is not to say that there are not people who mean to harm you and deceive you, because there are, and we should be alert and watch out for these people.

Again, nature provides us with a practical measure; you

know a good tree by the good fruit it produces. If you observe the fruit of someone's life, you will get a good idea of who they are as a person. The fruits that I have learned to look out for include people who consistently demonstrate humility, people who remain curious to learn, and people who are kind and brave enough to be vulnerable and show real empathy. This is good fruit.

It has been my experience that even in the most challenging situations, like exiting an organisation or relationship, we get to choose how we behave, even towards those whose actions have hurt us. I have learned that it is always better to take the high road in life. By this I mean we should say what we can that is positive, be encouraging without distorting the truth and always thank everyone we can thank. Small acts of kindness, especially during difficult times, make all the difference. It is possible to finish well and not burn bridges.

I remember a difficult situation I encountered when the senior leadership of an organisation decided to treat a group of committed and hard-working colleagues in a disrespectful and unprofessional way. This situation resulted in the group immediately leaving the organisation. I had a choice about how I conducted myself when I left. Whilst I was very disappointed, in private I offered the leaders some candid advice about the importance of always treating people with dignity and respect. In public, in front of the whole company, I chose to remind each colleague that it was an honour to get to do what they did and that the young people whose lives were impacted by their work mattered. It required their very best work. I thanked them for the opportunity to serve alongside them and then I moved on. We all have choices about how we leave teams, organisations or relationships. We can leave well.

The question that I have learned to ask at times like this is, "Are you more focused on your right to be treated well, or your responsibility to personally set the right example about how to treat people well?" Someone is always watching.

Leadership is not about making an impression; it is about making a difference. Is it communicating to people their worth and potential so well, that they believe it themselves?

The twenty-something learners came up with these insightful lessons about leading others:

So far in life, the lessons that I have learned about leading others have come from observing the experienced leaders in my life. Although it may sound simple, I do believe that the most important thing that you can do as a leader is to lead by example.

This is in my opinion the best way to set the standards for the whole team. The best leaders I have worked with, or observed from afar, have all held themselves to high standards, and been hard-working, honest, kind and accountable. By living by these principles they inspire and encourage others to do likewise, and this is how you align the team around a common purpose.

Accountability is never comfortable, but I have learned that a good rule of thumb for the leader is to take responsibility for things that go wrong and give recognition to their team members for what has worked well.

This creates the conditions for the team to be willing to take risks and make mistakes, which is how we all learn. Setting this example is empowering and lays the foundation that everyone on the team is encouraged to take ownership of their contribution, giving everyone the best chance of success.

Leading by example is very visible in sports teams. For example, South Africa's Siya Kolisi and Graeme Smith are both leaders who served their teams and did not expect anyone to do what they were not willing to do themselves. They demanded very high standards, but only after being willing to live up to those standards themselves and serve their teammates along the way.

One aspect of leading by example that I have learned from good leaders is that they do what they say they will do. When we keep our word, it builds trust in the team. This is how leaders gain the respect of their teams, by leading with integrity. Consistently doing what you say you will do is not easy, as life is complicated and always changing, but this might be one of the most important lessons for any leader to learn. People will judge you on what you do; not so much on what you say.

Following on from the lessons about leading yourself, which start with knowing yourself and in particular knowing your strengths and weaknesses, it is also important to be sufficiently open and vulnerable with your team. Admit your mistakes and be willing to speak about your struggles. This makes you real, and human and sets a good example for others to follow. Teams are by definition a collection of individuals who will bring a range of skills and experiences, which includes both strengths and weaknesses. The best teams can leverage one another's strengths and cover one another's weaknesses.

One additional lesson to add to this open and transparent approach is that mistakes are a necessary part of how we learn. I believe that leaders should allow colleagues to attempt new things and be willing to let them fail. Always stepping in to fix things or come up with a solution because of your many years of experience, does not always create a safe space for colleagues to "mess up." Good leaders are willing to take risks, which include allowing team members to learn and grow, sometimes through painful or costly failures.

Let your team make mistakes and avoid doing other people's jobs for them. Even if it is quicker in the short term, I think it is damaging over time as it does not allow each colleague to learn and grow. Your team will not keep progressing and it will likely risk undermining engagement and the motivation to give their very best. If the leader always solves each problem as it arises, then complacency will set in, or colleagues with the ambition to grow will simply move on to other organisations or teams.

I have learned that leading others on their journey of change does make life meaningful. I have had the opportunity to serve as a personal trainer and mentor, and two examples so far stand out on the power of leading others.

The first was how helping someone achieve their physical health goals led to a remarkable impact on all other aspects of their lives. The small changes led to the confidence to make broader changes, which impacted both his partner and his family. It reminded me to never underestimate the power of serving others as they make small changes towards the person they would like to become.

The second example taught me that leading others requires us to recognise the reality of where someone is in their life. This client was very unwell and in a place of despair. Building trust by walking each step of the road with them, offering them a sense of hope and purpose, reminding them of who they are and being there to see the choices they made was truly a privilege. Leading others does come at a price but to play a small part in someone else's journey and to see them now, thriving in life, is a reward of immense value.

An interesting lesson I have observed about leading others is that often the best leaders are the quiet ones. They are the ones who have learned to listen – to listen to others.

It seems that the historical leaders who are celebrated are those who were chosen to fight battles, subdue enemies and often achieve power, status and fortune. There are similar examples in modern times with the most visible leaders being those who appear to be seeking similar goals of power, status or wealth.

I have learned that these goals seem to miss the very real rewards of serving others, to playing a part in supporting someone else's growth and development. A quieter, more humble leader, who is genuinely interested in their team and who is kind and approachable, builds trust with those they are leading. This type of leader will ultimately have experience contributing to a team member's journey. Being quiet is not the same as not speaking the truth. I am learning that even when it is uncomfortable, there is a time to have the courage to stand up for what you believe and speak the truth.

Being a humble leader also supports your personal growth as you endeavour to keep developing.

As individuals we all have strengths and weaknesses — we have our good days and we all also have bad days. I am coming to learn that just because you may be the most experienced person in the room and you may be the leader in charge, it does not necessarily mean that you know what's best in all circumstances.

All of us can learn something from our team members. By endeavouring to be a lifelong learner, we will be less likely to enforce our opinions on colleagues or overpower them. Rather we can create an environment that brings the best out of everyone on the team.

> ***If you can see something that is not right, if injustice is clear to you, you can begin to imagine a better future.***

Chapter 6
Lessons about Leading Societal Change

"Somehow, things that once seemed impossible can seem inevitable. But the outcomes were not inevitable, someone decided to not accept the world as it is, but worked hard for what it should be."

– Condoleezza Rice

To help understand the lessons that I have learned on leading societal change, I should start with what I mean by societal change. I am referring to the changes that can take place to our social structures, the way we govern society, the institutions of the state, and of course our social norms and values. I include in societal change things that happen within local communities and up to national changes.

I am grateful to have seen first-hand one of our modern era's great examples of leading a peaceful social transformation. I was born in South Africa and, during my transition out of childhood; Nelson Mandela was eventually released from prison and he led the country through a period of extraordinary change. His example of leading "from the future" has convinced me that things do not need to remain as they are. Together we can choose to commit to making things a bit more like they should be.

As a young South African of European ethnic origin in the 1970s and 1980s, I had social privileges in terms of education and standing in society not given to the majority of my fellow South Africans. I have learned to never underestimate the transforming power of education. The truth is that it doesn't matter where you come from; it matters where you are going. I believe that we should aim to offer each child across the planet the gift of a good education.

I wrestled with the reality that I had been given a head-start in life, not because I had earned it or deserved it, but simply because of being born into the minority at that point in history. I was confronted with the truth of how my fellow South Africans had been treated. I had to settle in my own heart and mind what I believed to be right and wrong.

This understanding of the reality of life in South Africa emerged slowly for me. As a child, you absorb so much of the culture from the adults around you, but there comes a time when you have to take responsibility for what you believe. It took exposing myself to new voices and being willing to notice how the society I was living in was willing to treat people differently, simply because of their ethnicity. Seemingly small things were in reality profound signals of how human dignity was being systematically undermined. For example, language, like calling a grown man a "garden boy"; or a mature woman who worked in our home and cared for us, "the girl." I read the deeply moving novel by Alan Paton, 'Cry the Beloved Country' when I was about sixteen years old. It marked my heart and lifted before me a "mirror," which once I had seen it, I could not "un-see" the truth about apartheid in South Africa.

Based on the truth I found in the Bible, I believe that each one of us has intrinsic value and that we all deserve to be allowed to fulfil our potential. I made a choice that feelings of guilt over my start in life would be of little or no purpose. I decided to use the opportunities and education that I had been given to serve those who were not so fortunate. I decided to try to pay attention to the oppressed and those in need and work hard to offer more people the opportunity to fulfil their potential, wherever I was in the world.

It has been following this path in life that has given me lessons that I would like to share about leading societal change. It has been an honour to be asked to serve in roles which played a part in national-scale social reform programmes, including being part of changing the law of the land.

There are many important lessons that I learned from Nelson Mandela, but here are two that I would like to share. The first is that there is something about how we are made as humans, which appears unique among living creatures, that allows us to imagine a better future in our minds. We can create a vision of the future that does not yet exist, and then develop it and communicate it to other fellow humans. Then it is possible to lead a group of people towards making that future a reality.

Nelson Mandela believed that South Africa did not need to be defined by the differences amongst its citizens, but that it could celebrate the rich diversity of the country and that we could see ourselves as a "rainbow nation." A nation where each citizen was treated with dignity and respect and was given an equal opportunity to fulfil their potential.

The reality, when he set out this vision, was that the country was stuck in division and hatred. The existing political leaders had reinforced differences, especially ethnic divisions, as a way of amplifying fear in an attempt to cling to power. The undermining of human dignity and respect had become institutionalised. What made it so dangerous was that the full force of the state-backed it up. This is a sober reminder that democracy is not the same as freedom. It is possible to distort democracy to justify tyranny. In this case, it was the minority who exercised control over the majority, which was wrong, but it is worth remembering that the opposite would also be wrong. We should also guard against modern democratic systems where the majority exercises a kind of tyranny over minority groups. Freedom is only realised when we balance both the rights and responsibilities of the state and its citizens.

The powerful vision of freedom and unity set out by Mandela gave us hope and belief in the future. A new future in which all South Africans had their say, and their place, in a country that was stronger because of the rich diversity and resources of the nation.

The lesson that I have learned is that ordinary people can decide that we do not need to accept things as they are.

If you can see something that is not right, if injustice is clear to you, you can begin to imagine a better future.

The second lesson is about how we as individuals, families or even nations, can look forward despite the pain, suffering and trauma of the past. Under the leadership of Nelson Mandela and Archbishop Desmond Tutu, the country embarked on the remarkable journey of the "truth and reconciliation" commission. The principle behind this work was to expose the painful truth of the gross violations of human rights during South Africa's apartheid era, to provide the perpetrators with the opportunity to make full disclosure and to acknowledge what they had done before they could be granted amnesty. The independence of the commission gave it the credibility to carry out the difficult and painful task of shining light on this dark period of the country's history. As in any just process, the victims were given the proper respect and dignity to be heard. The victims were of course individuals and families, but so were communities and the nation as a whole. Before reconciliation and peace could be imagined, before healing could begin, the darkness needed to be expelled by light.

I listened to hours and hours of testimony from the commission and it changed something deep within me. I listened to stories about unthinkable trauma and abuse of fellow citizens. Now, nearly thirty years later, I am again in tears as I reflect on the weight of human tragedy that was laid bare. However, there was something much more powerful at work than the dark side of oppression and abuse; something more powerful than evil.

A close personal friend shared her direct experience of attending one of the "truth and reconciliation" meetings and kindly agreed for me to include it. This particular meeting was held in a huge tent, pitched in a field in Mannenberg on the "Cape Flats." This was a deprived area, dominated by violent gangs, and not somewhere a white middle-class woman would normally be found.

This is how she described the experience to me, "I had a strong conviction that this was the 'right thing to do', a conviction that outweighed my fears. The tent was packed and so I ended up standing. All these years later I can't remember many of the details, but what I vividly remember is what I experienced emotionally, spiritually and also physically.

We were asked to pair ourselves, as representatives of the 'oppressor' and the 'oppressed', with someone 'from the other side.' We spoke and we listened to each other. I listened to the real life of this lady, a domestic worker, with no higher education. I heard about her family and friends. I heard about the reality that I was shielded from by the state. My heart broke for this gentle lady. She found it hard to speak about some of the trauma she had experienced and I found it hard to listen to. We cried, each with our perspective, and our feelings, but we shared tears. We were guided to step into the gap as representatives and apologise for all the injustices they had suffered, explicitly and implicitly, as well as the distortions to their value as people. My heart was crushed with sadness for what she and her family, and so many others, had experienced. She held my hand and we were able to pray together. She forgave. It did not change the past, but it brought release. It was such a moving experience for both of us. It provided an opportunity for her to be heard and feel understood, and for me to listen. I heard more than the words she was saying, I got a glimpse of her heart and soul. We asked each other questions that we'd carried inside for years. More tears, more understanding, more asking for forgiveness and more forgiving.

We both left that tent that day feeling exhausted, but something powerful had happened. We were changed by each other."

You see, through the process of confession and truth-telling, a small glimmer of hope could emerge. Reconciliation is not an event; it is a process, and it requires the hard work of everyone getting involved and then slowly walking towards freedom.

I have tried to take the lessons I learned during this time and put them into practice.

Forgiveness is of course powerful at a personal level. Each one of us can follow the steps of confession, shining light on our mistreatment of others, and being willing to hear the weight of pain we cause. We can also choose to no longer carry this pain and bitterness into the future — to do the hard work of reconciliation. I know this to be true and very powerful. As a scientist, I am familiar with applying the laws of physics. I have come to learn that there are laws which could be described as "spiritual", like forgiveness. When applied, they work as powerfully as a physical law, such as gravity.

I have also experienced participating in a process of "forgiveness" between two large organisations. The leaders of the two organisations had been in a battle for many years, which had left a trail of mistrust and damage on both sides. Openly and transparently, in a courageous step, the two Chief Executives chose the path of confession. They stood in front of us, colleagues from both organisations and asked for forgiveness for the destructive behaviour on both sides. They committed to working toward an open and trusting relationship, united in a common purpose to make a positive difference in the lives of the people they served. Being part of this process reinforced my belief that there is wisdom in following the path of truth and reconciliation, to rebuild unity and learn once again to love and serve one another.

Later in life, after emigrating from South Africa to the United Kingdom, I was grateful to get to play a part in serving in Her Majesty's government as a civil servant. I have already mentioned that I worked within the prison and probation service. Having this "window" into life inside prisons, and the work of the probation service in communities reflected like a "mirror" some lessons that I had to wrestle with. I have often pondered the saying, "There, but for the grace of God, go I." It only takes a moment to make a poor decision and any one of us could get caught up in this system. In the fifteen years working in the justice system, I saw firsthand how a mature democracy wrestles with the rule of law, trying to keep the public safe and how it treats some of the most damaged and marginalised citizens.

I have learned firsthand that things do not need to stay as they are. If we can imagine a better future we can, together, start to do the work to make things a little bit more like they should be.

By now, you will be familiar with my belief that it helps to start from the position of a curious learner. Leading societal change is no different.

As part of my introduction to the justice system in England and Wales, I started by pondering the treatment of the socially excluded in the Bible. The list in the Bible includes people who are in severe poverty, people who have nowhere suitable to live, people who do not have suitable clothes to wear and people whose family lives have broken down. It includes the unemployed, those who are very ill – whether due to their physical or their mental health – and those who have a dependence on drugs or alcohol. It includes those who are refugees or foreigners, having fled their country looking for a safe place to call home. This list then concludes with the instruction to also visit those who are in prison. The Bible describes these people as "the least of these." It calls those who serve "the least of these", good. For the avoidance of doubt, the description "least of these" is not a belittling or patronising term. Rather, it is an acknowledgement of how little these people have and how they have been treated so far.

As someone who had seen real poverty in my childhood in Africa I could understand why, when describing the socially excluded, you might include the poor, the homeless, the unemployed, the uneducated, the ill and the displaced. I was less clear about why you would add to this list "those in prison."

If your understanding of prison is the place a society puts the citizens who have each made an individual choice to break the law or to harm another citizen and must therefore bear individual and sole responsibility for their actions, then why would you include these people on a list like this? My exposure to the reality of how countries deploy prison systems, especially wealthy Western nations, is that this is where the most socially disadvantaged, excluded and damaged people are found. If you are looking for the "least of these", then in most countries you will find them in disproportionate numbers in prisons. The ancient wisdom from the Bible to visit those in prison is profound. It is a reminder to every generation to seek out those pushed to the margins of society. We should offer them the help and support they need to begin a journey of reintegration and inclusion into society, for their sake, for their children's sake and all our sake.

It is no surprise that wise thinkers have made how a country treats those in prison, or how we treat foreigners seeking refuge in our country, a measure of the civilisation of a society. If the bonds that hold each one of us within a set of social norms, in terms of how we treat one another, are strained, broken, or never established when we were children, then we should not be surprised if people live outside of society's norms. It takes a whole community to raise a child. If a child has not been raised to live within boundaries, to be accepted and to belong, then we should not be surprised if that person struggles to live within the laws of the land.

It is also, of course, very important to train a child how to do what is right and how to search for truth. As a society, we share the responsibility for what has happened in the lives of the people who end up in our prisons.

The question that formed in my heart was, "What would it take to ensure that every woman or man leaving prison in England and Wales was offered help and support upon their release?"

I embarked on a learning journey to understand as much as I could about the needs of the people in prison. I studied the evidence base. I worked with organisations and people with lived experience of the system, to offer help and support to those leaving prison. I got to work with some of the world's leading academics and professionals, in the field of criminology. I am grateful to have worked with colleagues in the prison and probation service who understood and shaped the global evidence about "what works" in behaviour change interventions. As is so often the case, some of the most profound and practical insights I gained were by listening to the real people in prison doing the hard work of making this change happen in their lives.

Proximity to the "least of these" is still one of the most important ways to discover truth. I was regularly humbled by the practical wisdom of people who were navigating the prison system – a system which struggles with balancing the need for security, necessary to keep people safe, and the need for kindness and compassion. It's a system that tries to provide the necessary support for those who have endured great pain and trauma, even if they too have caused great pain and trauma to others.

The cumulative insights from so many were pulled together into a vision of improving the support people were given as they left prison, and the ambition to help each reintegrate into society. This vision was refined into a plan with the help and support of colleagues, many of whom became good friends over five years. In ways that I cannot take credit for, this work culminated in changing the law in England and Wales through a bill known as the "Offender Rehabilitation Act 2014."

This Act of Parliament introduced a statutory obligation on the state to plan for and provide post-release supervision and support for each person leaving prison in England and Wales. No legislation is perfect, and the implementation of national-scale changes comes with considerable challenges, both financially and operationally. However, this was another small shift towards acknowledging that change is hard and we all at times need help and support.

A just justice system upholds the rule of law; it sets fair boundaries for all citizens to ensure that we do not harm one another. It sets fair punishment for those who break the law. The pain and suffering caused to both victims of crime and their families can be devastating, leaving them with life-changing trauma and pain. Ultimately they deserve justice. It is also true that a just justice system should acknowledge that citizens need to be included, supported and restored to find a place to belong in society. We all need to experience being loved to learn to love.

I have spent a great deal of time thinking about issues of justice. I have asked myself questions like, "What would a just justice system look like?" and "Is there a better way than our current punitive approach to criminal justice?"

These are big questions with no simple answers, so I offer just a few thoughts for the curious learners among you.

It appears as though justice systems around the world find it more straightforward to exercise control over the poor and the marginalised. They are much less effective in holding the rich and powerful to account. They prioritise prosecuting the socially excluded for crimes associated with poverty, which are often perpetrated to cope with their pain, suffering and trauma.

I do, of course, acknowledge that these crimes are anti-social and cause real harm to local communities.

In contrast, a much broader consideration of the harm caused by very large corporations or powerful, wealthy individuals may conclude that some of the intergenerational harms caused by some of their actions may far outweigh acquisitive crime or antisocial behaviour. I am not suggesting that breaking the law is acceptable in either case. I am simply saying that if you can accumulate sufficient wealth, power and influence, you can afford to lobby governments to create rules and laws. Laws which allow you or your organisation to technically steer just inside the law of the land, to make permissible certain actions that turn out to cause long-term harm. This makes it much less likely that you will be held to account for your actions.

However, those who suffer the most from systemic injustice seem to always be the poorest and the most marginalised. I am sure that there is a better way.

I would argue that lessons from the Bible remind us that justice calls us to radical generosity to the poor, a relentless commitment to creating more equal opportunities for all fellow humans and to advocate for the poor and the weak. This might give us a clue to finding a better way.

What I have learned about leading societal change is to start with what moves your heart. Start with where you notice injustice. That is a good place to focus your energy on making things better.

Whatever conclusion you may have reached about your purpose on earth, I have learned that all through history there were people who saw what was required in their generation, and they chose to act.

Take the time to learn as much as you can about the things that move you, and then find opportunities to get close to those impacted by what you can see and feel, to ground your understanding in reality. I am an applied scientist by training, and intellectual insight alone does not deliver real societal change. We need to turn these insights into action. A vision of a better world, or a better life for one person, is not going to become a reality until someone dares to act.

You can start where you are, with the resources you already have at your disposal and with the people you have around you, and you can simply take a small step. This is all that I did, with the people around me. The doors that then opened, the support of colleagues, friends and family, and with what was a Divine guiding hand that I cannot fully explain. It was possible to ask the question, "What if we could make a difference?" This started a process that ultimately resulted in a change to the law of the land.

The belief of faith in a better future starts with what is not yet seen until the thing that was once deemed impossible ends up being something you see happening before your eyes.

The reward of faith in the unseen is to see the change in reality. It is true that ordinary people, doing what is right, can later see things that seem extraordinary.

I have been infuriated at the injustice experienced by both victims and their families, as well as some perpetrators of crimes. I have been in tears at the depth of pain and trauma I encountered. If you still think that the distinction between victim and perpetrator is simple, you may not have had the opportunity to look deep enough into the brokenness and chaos of the lives and backgrounds of the damaged people caught up in our justice systems.

I have also been humbled to see the level of commitment and perseverance from the people who work for HM Prison and Probation Service. They should rightly be described as modern-day heroes. I have encountered so many powerful, personal stories about how someone was willing to come alongside the life of a person who had lost hope. We can hold on to the hope of someone who has lost hope. We can remind them of their life purpose, their hopes and dreams, so that slowly over time they may once again find hope.

Social change is something that starts in our hearts. With broken hearts, we can humbly ask the question, "In what small way could I help to make things a little better?"

Could you hold on to hope for someone while they slowly re-find their way?

Every life matters, every life is worthy and capable of greatness. You never know how your small part in helping someone might turn out to be the key that unlocks their potential. They may go on to impact the lives of many.

Sometimes the most "spiritual" thing that you can do for someone is to meet their immediate physical and material needs. Even when things seem rather bleak, and a way forward seems unimaginable, remember that it is in the midst of unprecedented challenges that we find unprecedented opportunities to make a positive impact.

We can all ask ourselves bold questions like; "What am I doing to tear down the systemic injustice in our society?

This is what the twenty-something learners said when I asked about leading societal change:

The truthful response to this question is, as a twenty-something-year-old, that I am not confident that I have sufficient insight at this time to contribute any lessons on leading societal change. Perhaps in a few decades, I will have lessons of my own to share.

From what I have observed so far, making meaningful change in the world is something that takes time, commitment and a lot of patience. It certainly isn't easy. We only have to observe the world around us, either on the news or in our communities, to see that those with power can so easily be driven by negative motives.

It has also often felt to me that as a young adult, not in an obvious position of power to make major societal change, there is very little I can personally contribute.

However, the truth is that each of us has the power to make small changes, even big changes, simply by taking those first steps in the right direction. Some of history's most influential leaders of societal change did not come from positions of power, but instead made the choice to do what was right; not what was easy. Often, it seems, at great sacrifice to themselves. Malala Yousafzai is a great modern-day example.

It may not happen overnight but, as the next generation, we have a responsibility to not ignore the things that make us angry, sad or that we simply see as unjust. We must find ways to start learning, engaging and being the voice for change in our world.

When I think about how we can continue to make the world a better place, it appears to me that we need to find a way to bring people together. If we can align those who come from very different social groups but have shared values and goals, we can create a force for good that can drive positive social change.

Put simply, generosity changes lives.

Chapter 7
Lessons on Stewardship and Generosity

"Where your treasure is, there your heart will be also."

– Matthew 6:21

So far we have shared lessons about learning in and of itself, as well as lessons about leadership. In this section, we would like to share a few lessons on what matters; things that have eternal value.

I am confident that these lessons are well worth exploring for any serious, curious learner.

The first of these truths relates to what I understand as one of the main purposes of humanity on planet Earth. I have learned from studying the ancient wisdom in the Bible that we are on this planet as stewards, to care for the earth and one another, and to join in with the incredible design of the natural world to live within its rhythms and its ways. The origin of the universe, including our planet, would have been chaotic. As good stewards, we can use our divine gifts and talents to begin to bring order to this beautiful and often wild planet.

We can imagine and create new things and new ways of thinking and, if we align with the truth and the right divine order, we can play our part in bringing about real progress towards human thriving. If we are truly good stewards and are willing to respect all living things, we can work together with the natural world to live in the abundance that it can provide.

If, however, we choose to exercise our stewardship in a way that stores up as much "treasure" for ourselves as possible, we are driven by greed and selfish gain. If we become so arrogant that we see ourselves as better than other people, and all other creatures, then we begin to damage and exploit. This way could eventually destroy the very planet we call home.

You cannot serve two masters. If you are serving yourself, to get as much as you can from others and the earth, then you cannot be serving others and serving the greater good. Each one of us needs to choose who we will serve. If we serve our wealth and possessions and our fame, we are serving something temporary and it will perish.

Taking the money always comes at a price, and the price is that it changes you.

The more I come to understand the intricate design of each living creature, including ourselves, the more I believe that we were designed to live in beautiful harmony. We were designed to live in harmony with each person and each creature and the natural systems at work across the earth, with each playing a unique and important part towards the abundant life on earth.

It is evident that one of the major challenges we face is how to sustain our ever-growing need for reliable and clean energy; to keep up the progress we have made towards human thriving.

Fossil fuels have contributed enormously to the progress we have made, but we have also come to better understand the price we have paid for using these sources of fuel. Real progress is now being made in terms of renewable technology. However, I wonder whether once again the natural world has pointed the way to a solution. The sun is a shining example of almost unlimited energy. Using the power of the sun to generate energy is already making an important contribution to renewable energy. What if we can take one more step towards an abundance of clean energy for the entire planet, by learning the lessons of the nuclear fusion reactions which power the sun?

If we solve the technological challenge of nuclear fusion, imagine how much more progress we could make towards an abundant life on Earth for all living things.

One simple example of stewardship is thinking carefully about the food we eat. I am learning that what we choose to put in our bodies matters to our health and well-being. It is how we show that we love and respect our physical bodies. The discipline to make healthy choices will require saying no to easy or comforting choices in the short term. It is also true that the choices we make as consumers either help the shift towards better stewardship of the planet or continue to support unsustainable agricultural practices.

I have become particularly curious about our stewardship of the land, including the actual soil. The soil is a combination of organic and inorganic chemicals. Plants need these chemicals for growth. If we regard the soil as a resource that we can exploit for our gain, to take from it and not put back what it needs, we then discover that we lose the healthy soil through erosion and end up with barren land.

The truth about the soil, especially healthy soil untouched by human over-use, is that it contains an amazing array of life. It is designed to be a thriving ecosystem with millions of intricately connected living organisms each playing their part in sustaining life on earth. It is easier perhaps to understand more visible ecosystems, such as the wildlife on the plains of Africa or tropical jungles. However, if we look below the surface of the soil, there is an even more rich and diverse world of living creatures. If we are willing to shift our focus from taking from the soil or overworking the land, we will find that it can be restored to its healthy and productive state.

There is an emerging field of science called "regenerative" or "restorative" agriculture. This is not new but is ancient wisdom about treating the land and animals with the respect that they deserve. It is about planning for the land to rest and recover. The truth is that stewardship of the land mirrors similar principles in all walks of life. We need to allow the land to rest to restore the microbiology of the soil and disrupt any imbalances in terms of parasites and pests. It is about not taking everything we can from the land but, rather, being generous and leaving any excess of food for others. This will inevitably impact economic measures, like short-term profits, but it is more sustainable in the longer term.

The impact of large-scale commercial agriculture has become clearer over my lifetime. Whilst humanity has significantly improved levels of food production across the world, it has come at a significant cost. Large corporations now dominate agricultural production. This ever-increasing drive for more profits has had real consequences for the land and the communities living on it.

Modern commercial farming methods have become major global contributors to deforestation, desertification, water contamination and soil degradation. We continue to lose vast amounts of topsoil across the planet each year through our farming practices. By planting vast quantities of the same single crop year after year, and overgrazing our land, we have not been good stewards of the land.

To bring the lesson of stewardship to life, I thought I'd very briefly explain two examples of "regenerative" agriculture that I have personally encountered. The first is an approach to land preparation, which is called "no tilling." Tilling is the agricultural preparation of soil by mechanical agitation of various types. The second is "regenerative grazing."

"No-till" farming is designed to improve the healthy functioning of the soil and all the living organisms within it. Healthy soil should be full of living organisms, which are helpful to plants. These organisms perform many functions. For example, some of them attach nitrogen from the air and make it accessible to plants. Some help to trap and hold water in the soil and others aerate and loosen the soil to increase water absorption. This enables the plant's roots to grow deeper. In this farming method, a diverse layer of plants is grown and crops are rotated regularly. A "cover" for the soil is maintained at all times to protect its living organisms from the sun and the weather.

The biodiversity above and below the soil also drives a much healthier ecosystem. In healthy soil, there should be many more organisms below the ground than what we see above the ground. In traditional commercial farming, the soil is ploughed and tilled rigorously to leave bare earth. This is what I remember from my childhood as farmers proudly prepared plant-free land. The problem with this approach is that it kills or damages many of the living organisms. Without natural insects to protect plants, you need to spray pesticides to protect the plants. Many of these chemicals then leech into the waterways or kill the living organisms or insects necessary for healthy living soil – not to mention the impact on important pollinators like bees.

By treating the soil as a living ecosystem, and caring for it in the way we farm, the evidence is now showing that the soil can return to levels of health and productivity not seen for generations.

I find this very hopeful and could reframe the purpose of farming into the practice of being "stewards of the soil." The crops and animals are just playing their part in managing the land. This might be a healthier and more sustainable way of thinking about the land. As someone who also believes in the importance of our oceans, learning to steward the world's oceans similarly is going to be equally important.

The second example is "regenerative grazing." Scientists studying vast herds of wild animals, such as the wildebeest herds in central Africa, have discovered that it is possible to raise animals intensively and reduce the impact on the land.

High-volume commercial animal production is contributing to greenhouse gas emissions, deforestation and overgrazing, soil degradation and desertification. However, if better practices are used it is possible to sequester vast amounts of carbon from the atmosphere by allowing the grasses to grow and replenish our soils over time. In regenerative grazing the animals are moved regularly through the grasses, like you would see on the plains of Africa, never overgrazing and allowing enhanced plant growth. The animals trample plant matter and their dung into the soil, restoring biomass and feeding the living organisms in the soil. This replenishes topsoil rather than degrading or eroding it.

A gentle reminder for all of us is that, despite much of humanity now living in urban areas, every one of us depends on the productivity of the land for our daily food.

Our social systems are connected to our ecological systems. We have already seen how we, as humans, are the biggest cause of animal extinction as we destroy natural habitats. This has not been good stewardship of the earth.

The natural world is clearly "groaning" under the weight of human impact instead of thriving from the good we can do.

We humans certainly appear to have impacted things like the climate, water quality and soil health, plus we have contributed to deforestation and a loss of biodiversity. The earth is our home and, because of our actions, it is now damaged. The root causes of much of the harm are likely to be found in our human weaknesses. These certainly include selfishness, greed and even apathy. This list of human frailties has also increased inequality of opportunity and injustice.

In a culture driven by what we can get quickly, of seeking pleasure and comfort, we think that we can simply "throw away" what we've used and move on. We forget that there is no place called "away" on the earth. What we dispose of on Earth stays on Earth. We might bury or hide our waste, but it is still here on Earth. It is being stored up for later generations to deal with.

It is also the case that poverty and loss of biodiversity are inextricably linked. The truth is that the world's poorest are impacted the most by the damage we are doing to the earth. If we are going to take seriously our responsibility as stewards of the earth, we need to take seriously the pain and suffering caused by not looking after the planet for the poorest and the marginalised.

We can all play our part, in some small way, in restoring the planet so every living thing can thrive on the earth.

I have had the opportunity to work for a range of businesses, both large and small. What I have observed is that the short-term demands from the shareholders, to deliver increased profitability, are not always aligned with long-term sustainability. As leaders, we should ask the difficult questions about how we are balancing short-term profits for the shareholders, with the broader impact on the lives of people and communities in which we operate. Without a fair return on investment, the business is likely to no longer exist. However, neither employees, their communities, nor the environment, should be exploited whilst generating this wealth. To leave the world a bit better than we found it, will require a more holistic understanding of shareholder and public value.

This might be one of those moments in human history where those of us who can see the truth, who are willing to re-learn ancient lessons, could take a stand on behalf of all living creatures; to start the hard work of becoming better stewards of the earth.

Stewardship of the earth is, of course, our shared responsibility as humanity. However, I would also like to share some more personal lessons about stewardship as individuals or families.

I believe that the more we are given, or the more we have, the greater the responsibility we must bear. Being a faithful steward of what you have, starts with how well you manage small things.

Our finances are a great place to start to learn to be good stewards. This can start as children, with our pocket money or our allowance, if we are fortunate enough to get these. We can also do this with what we earn from our paid work. These are a few of the lessons that I have learned, from the ancient wisdom in the Bible, which have served me well in terms of financial stewardship for over four decades.

Firstly, I have learned to acknowledge that what I earn is a result of more than my efforts. There is a Source greater than me. I have learned to share a proportion of what I earn as my first act of stewardship. Sharing a predetermined percentage of your income to serve a greater need may seem counterintuitive, but I have tested this truth and proven that it simply works. There are of course many people on the planet who barely earn enough to survive. For them, their gift may be very small or something in kind, by sharing in other ways.

We will return to the principle of generosity, but there is a powerful freedom that comes from first sharing some of our income with others before spending it on ourselves.

It is important to decide what you have to share in advance, and then share it, nothing more and nothing less. Share it joyfully because it is what you have decided to do. Once you have shared some of your earnings, it is then wise to ensure that you set aside some money for savings. Save to support a longer-term dream or ambition, and to build up a sensible buffer for life's inevitable surprises. I recognise that saving money is a challenge for many people across the world, but it is sound wisdom to not spend everything you earn.

In our Western societies, we treat savings as our own, but there are cultures across the world that have retained strong community values and who share what they have with anyone in need. There is deep wisdom in this approach which puts the needs of others first.

If you adjust your standard of living to always be at the level of what you can afford to spend, after sharing and saving, then your financial stewardship will be more sustainable.

When the opportunity arises to invest, remember to invest in trees rather than in fruit. This is a reminder that investing is best viewed through a long-term lens. If you put your money into fruit you can enjoy it and you can sell it. However, if you invest in trees and look after your investments, then they will produce fruit on an ongoing basis.

These are not complicated lessons. I can confirm from my personal experience that if you apply them in a disciplined way, over many decades, you will see the rewards. It is never too soon to start. Ancient wisdom from the Bible points out that being a good and faithful steward, of what you have over a lifetime, then allows you to leave an inheritance to your children's children. I am not suggesting that leaving a financial legacy for our children, and their children, is what is most important. A legacy should be living. The lessons we share and the example we give to those who follow after us are much more valuable than any amount of money we may leave.

The truth is that one day we will all be asked to give an account of what we did with what we were given. So these financial stewardship principles do not only apply to money but also to our talents and our influence.

Returning to the topic of generosity, I have learned that this is one of the defining characteristics of someone good.

Put simply, generosity changes lives.

When we are generous to others, especially to those who have no way of repaying our generosity, you will find that it connects us to people in a way that nothing else can.

Living a life of generosity with your time, your energy and your resources, helps each one of us align ourselves with what matters. One of the surprising things about sharing what you have is how it frees our hearts.

Remember, whatever you give to someone can never be stolen from you.

I have observed over many decades that organisations and businesses that maintain a culture of secrecy, carefully hold on to their ideas and treat everyone as a threat, tend to perform worse than those who choose trust and openness. There is something very attractive about organisations that are generous with their time and support, who collaborate and contribute to making a difference.

It is something that I have seen done well in the start-up world, where entrepreneurs understand the importance of building networks and being willing to help fellow start-ups. This willingness to be open, and to positively support each other's success, is in my view a very healthy example of how we can achieve more together.

Generosity extends beyond our resources, it is also a choice we make in terms of how we treat those around us. I have learned that it is more helpful to those around me, to assume positive intent. Rather than assuming the worst, I start with believing in the good in my colleagues. I seek to try to understand what has happened before jumping to accusation or judgment. This kind of generosity of heart starts with a belief in people and errs on the side of kindness and goodness. These small choices are how trust is grown.

Closely related to the idea of giving generously, is this question about how to wisely respond to "free" stuff. The lesson that I have learned in this regard is that nothing of value is "free." Getting something for nothing is a myth.

When an organisation offers you something for free, don't be deceived by this. As the saying goes, "There is no such thing as a free lunch." For example, if a company offers you a "free" email service, it is because access to your data is worth so much more to them than what you would pay for the service. Your attention and your data are the price that you are paying, as they can sell that to advertisers.

We need to learn to be sceptical about "free" offers because they always come at a cost; your time, attention and focus. "Shiny things" that distract us, can take us off the intentional course we set regarding the person we aim to become.

For the avoidance of doubt, this lesson about "free stuff" should not be confused with someone actually offering you real generosity and kindness. When you encounter someone who offers you a kind gift, with no expectation of anything in return, then I have learned that it is wise to graciously accept the gift and "suffer the kindness."

I have seen and heard countless examples from very poor communities of families offering the best food that they have to strangers, despite their own family having to go without a proper meal. This is because of their deep-rooted commitment to kindness, hospitality and generosity. If you are ever in the fortunate position to receive this kind of gift, respect the sacrifice and even if it hurts your pride to not reciprocate, "suffer the kindness." This is how you honour the gift-giver.

Being a faithful steward and living a life of generosity is like building your life on a solid foundation. It is wise to choose to "build" with precious materials like gold, silver and costly stones, rather than building with wood, straw and mud. When you find your life subjected to the inevitable storms of life or the refining fires that come to test us, a life built on the truth will become more pure and more valuable, rather than be ruined.

The twenty-something learners have valuable lessons to add regarding stewardship and generosity:

I believe that certain practices, which may at first glance appear to be counterintuitive, can be of huge benefit to people. Examples of these practices are loving your neighbour as yourself, setting time apart to rest from work each week (the practice of Sabbath from the Scriptures), being generous with our money and giving to people in need.

A particular example of this from the Bible is to give a "tithe" (a tenth) of your earnings to the church to serve those in need. At the outset, this may not appear to make mathematical or economic sense, but I have come to believe that if you put this into practice, it does produce real benefits to not only the receiver and their community but also to the giver over time. These practices may not all yet have the clarity of thorough scientific explanations but it does not mean that they are not true, they may be some of the most real truths we know.

Generosity is something that can often get misconstrued as a transactional process, given to get something back in return. Changing this mindset to make generosity a part of the way that we live our lives is so important, not to get anything back but to give joyfully to others, just because we can. I have also learned that generosity is so much more than just financial. I think that giving someone your time might be the most important thing you can give. I am very fortunate, and grateful, to have a father-in-law who is very generous with his time; to listen to my ideas and struggles. Giving our time to others reminds them of how valuable they are to us.

Watching those whom I have grown up around who are intentionally generous, it is easy to see the impact this has had on their relationships and social interactions. So many lives are touched by even small gestures.

Whilst generosity is often thought about in the context of financial gifts, often I have seen that some of the most generous people I know give far more than just their money. Giving our time, and skills or just being a listening ear during a difficult time is just as valuable as our finances.

What I learned during the recent pandemic was that thinking about your local community is matters important. This includes caring for those in your neighbourhood, but it also includes thinking about your choices in terms of how you spend your money.

During the pandemic, being able to support local farmers and shops was one small way that I was reminded of how we all play a part in making our society work. I have continued this practice in small ways where I can, for example buying honey from local farmers, which does cost a lot more than the big brands from the supermarkets. This keeps local shops in business and has the added benefit of maintaining healthy bee populations, which are so vital to our ecosystem and food production.

We can all choose to make small, kind gestures to those in our lives and our community.

We should work "from" a place of rest, not "for" it.

Chapter 8
Lessons on Rest and the Rhythms of Life

"We should try to ruthlessly eliminate hurry from our lives."

– Dallas Willard

If stewardship and generosity are lessons about our purpose, these next lessons are about how we are designed to live in harmony with all life on earth. I am learning that we are designed to function within the rhythms of the natural world – days, weeks and seasons. If we aim to thrive, I believe that we are more likely to experience a full and contented life if we learn to live within these rhythms.

I wonder whether we need to re-learn the importance of rest. We live such busy and distracted lives that it has become necessary to intentionally commit to ruthlessly eliminate distraction and hurry from our lives. We have embraced a narrative that we have to strive to get ahead and to work long hours. We feel that if we put in enough work, we might earn the right to have a short break and to rest from our labour.

What I am coming to learn is that whilst it is true that work is good for us, and meaningful work does improve our health and well-being, we might just have work and rest the wrong way around. If I study the ancient wisdom from the Bible, to learn about the rhythms of life according to our original design, it teaches that we should work "from" a place of rest, not "for" it.

The world of work is changing quickly. Technological disruption to work in the next few decades is likely to exceed any disruption seen in human history so far. The adoption of technology, to automate work, has produced significant increases in productivity and increased output across the global economy. With the arrival of the information revolution, we are creating machines that can outperform humans in cognitive as well as physical work. The debate about whether the machines we are creating will achieve a level of general intelligence remains unanswered. What is certainly already the case is that our human ability to explain how machines are analysing information, and rapidly increasing in capability to perform "human-like" functions, is already beyond our ability to simply explain.

In a world where machines can do most of the so-called "boring work" and do it so efficiently that the costs are very low, we will need to rethink the meaning and purpose of work. Do we work because it gives us meaning or is it more likely that our work simply serves the purpose of providing income? How will these technological shifts impact the global economy and the distribution of wealth across the planet? Can this powerful new technology be used as a force for good? For example by transforming education by giving every child easy access to their own expert "digital tutor" to guide their learning journey, while still connecting them to real human teachers.

I do not have simple answers to these questions but, so far, many of the ways that we have deployed technology in the information age appear to have added to our sense of "busyness." This has produced a more distracted and stressed state of humanity.

Machines are not living creatures like humans, and whatever happens, our true sense of meaning and purpose is found in our relationships with real people. Perhaps it is time for us to begin to take it seriously, returning to our more natural rhythms of life, relationships and rest. We should put these powerful new tools in their rightful place in the service of humanity. Machines can certainly augment our capability but they are in the end just machines that we have created.

I, like many others, have fallen into the "busyness" trap over my career, working long hours and not always having the discipline to slow down. I have learned, as have other wise apprentices of Jesus, that the busier I get, the more time I need to take to pause, rest and pray.

Rest is how to realign our hearts, minds and bodies with the unforced rhythms of grace – the gift of life that we each receive when we are born. Rest is something that we can find for our souls.

If we start each week according to what the Bible would call a "Sabbath day" – a day when we do not work – we avoid participating in consumer activities. Rather we celebrate the beauty of life and connect with those we love most. We get to do the recreational things we enjoy and see our wonderful place in creation. We rest.

This first day of the week is a kind of re-ordering of what it means to be truly free. By forming this habit we are choosing to allow our souls to be restored, putting our trust in something (or Someone) greater than ourselves. This is how to train ourselves to be content with what we have and to pay attention to the important relationships in our lives.

I believe that this is what "intentional stopping" looks like. This kind of rest is not passive. I am coming to see it more like letting our roots grow deep into the Source of life, and not putting undue confidence in our ability to make things better by simply working harder.

There is a deep humility to this kind of rest. If we ignore the wisdom of taking time each week to rest, and if we try to live on all work and no rest, we will find that eventually, our bodies will force us into unplanned rest or illness. We need to honour and respect our design and not ignore our limitations.

In the short term, the greatest punishment for not taking time to "Sabbath" each week is that we miss out on the beauty of "Sabbath" rest. We pay the price in ways that we don't fully understand. As we discussed in lessons about leading yourself, if you orient your life to focus only on what you can achieve, you might miss the deeper wisdom of discovering who you are becoming.

Being should come before doing.

There is of course a shorter cycle than a weekly rhythm, which is the daily rhythm. Sleep is emerging as being even more important, to our health and wellbeing, than we have ever understood. I would encourage any curious learner to take the time to study all the incredible new insights emerging into the powerful biological processes that take place when we sleep. Learn how getting a good quality night's sleep is now understood to be one of the most important ways to improve our mental and physical health.

Sleep plays an essential role in our metabolism, our immune system and our overall brain health. Every cell in our body is connected to the twenty-four-hour rhythm. Each positive change we make to our sleep patterns impacts our health down to the genetics of our cells. New cells are continually being made each day.

To be the best we can be for those around us, and to offer others the best version of ourselves, we owe it to them and ourselves to take sleep seriously.

Working "from rest" rather than "for rest" starts with a good night's sleep.

Like all life habits, getting a consistently good night's sleep takes discipline and practice. It requires deciding when you should sleep rather than when you feel the need to sleep. It requires keeping consistent sleep patterns, adjusting light and temperature, removing distractions like our phones and not preloading our minds with unhelpful thoughts before we go to sleep. What we think about last thing before we go to sleep, and first thing when we wake in the morning, may be the most important and formative thoughts going through our minds.

After a refreshing sleep, the new day starts with each morning filled with potential. We face each new day afresh, asking, 'What is today going to bring?' One of our core freedoms in life is to choose how we will face each day.

Then at the end of the day, when it is over, the day has become whatever it was going to be. It is not new anymore; it has come to an end. We have lived that day and we can take time to remember the events of the day and prepare for the following day. I have learned that it is wise to analyse the day. I choose to do this through prayer. To be grateful for what was good, to repent of things that went wrong, and to trust with hope for a new day. When we glean what we can from the day and put both the negative and positive lessons into perspective, we try to orient ourselves to a better future. A future which puts the highest truth in its rightful place. Then, once again, we rest.

There is wisdom in paying attention to the rhythms of a day, a week and a season. If we work hard and do our best during the day, then set a finishing line when work stops, we can say "That is enough for today." The same principle applies to a week, a season and a year. Finishing lines not only bring the satisfaction of closure, but importantly they set boundaries. We need boundaries in our crazy busy world more than ever before. I have learned that without these boundaries, one day, one week or one season rolls into the next.

One way to think about this principle of enforced rest and recreation is that it is like the advice you get on an aeroplane. In the event of a sudden loss of air pressure, please fit your oxygen mask before helping others. We all need the space, the air to breathe, to be our best for those around us.

"Busyness" robs us of the time to be kind.

Living with no margin in life leaves us with no margin to stop and notice someone in need, or to pause in wonder at the beauty around us.

One important lesson that I am learning, after many decades, is that if you find yourself with less time available, pause more. Our schedules should be far less about what we need to get done, than about the person we want to become.

Training ourselves in the practice of pausing, silence and solitude, is like an invitation to find those pathways into the deepest places of our being; to find freedom and our authentic selves. This is much less about "feeling good" than "being good."

A gentle warning to those of us driven to high performance and achievement: Trying to measure the successful outcome of your practices of silence and solitude is unwise. Simply continuing to practice times of silence and solitude without distraction is enough. Just keep doing it. I understand this as a process of surrender.

You do not add the practice of solitude to a busy life. Rather, solitude is about removing and simplifying. It is subtracting things to find space to rest and breathe. It is the right thing to do for our souls and it is good.

Regarding resting, these are the lessons that the twenty-somethings have to share:

In today's culture, we have become so strongly focused on success that often it feels that we glorify working hard at all costs. It is too easy to find myself over-committing, working longer hours than planned, and ultimately getting much less time for rest. Although this is often with good intentions, to help colleagues or progress with important projects, this constant giving without sufficient rest eventually can lead to burnout.

It can be challenging to find a healthy balance between giving your best effort and giving too much of yourself. Being mindful and actively asking ourselves this question regularly, as well as learning to recognise the early signs of burnout within ourselves, can help us to work more sustainably. Looking after your well-being might just be the best thing you can do not only for yourself but for your relationships with family, friends and colleagues.

What I have learned about resetting the rhythm of my body, is that I need good sleep and I need to work hard both physically and mentally. I have found that if my brain is tired from mentally challenging tasks, then my body gets restless and sends me the signal that I need to move and do something physically challenging. If I have exercised hard, but not engaged my brain much that day, then there is a real risk that my brain starts to "wander" at night and this can impact my quality of sleep.

We all have our human limitations and we should respect these boundaries, both physically and mentally. Overdoing your physical training, to the point of causing injury, will certainly mean that you will not rest well as you will be in pain and require a period of recovery. Finding the right rhythms in life is key to being properly rested.

Learning to shift our feelings about rest from something that makes us less dedicated or even lazy to being something positive and necessary for our overall success, is essential. Rest not only allows us to physically recharge but also gives us time to reflect and refocus on our goals, which can be difficult to do when running full steam ahead.

I have always thought about learning as an intentional process, like reading a book, listening to a podcast or lecture, or practising a new skill. What modern science is starting to reveal is that much of our learning happens during times of rest and recovery.

When we sleep, especially during deep sleep, it appears as though our brains can reallocate resources to process thoughts and lessons from the day. This turns out to play an essential role in our ability to learn. So the lesson that I am learning is that the quality and duration of our sleep are directly connected to the lessons we learn in life.

This is definitely something I am curious to learn more about.

> *I have learned that our humble hearts are more helpful and can teach us so much more than our proud minds.*

Chapter 9
Lessons on Humility and Gratitude

"Humility is not thinking less of yourself; it's thinking of yourself less."

– C.S. Lewis

I have already described what I have learned about stewardship and generosity as lessons about our purpose, and rest as a foundational practice of how we can learn to live well. So now, let's turn to the lessons that I have learned about humility and gratitude.

I would describe these as how best to position our hearts. I have come to know that humility is the pathway to wisdom and to living a life of integrity and wholeness.

With humble hearts, we are best positioned to practice gratitude, which I have discovered is the pathway to happiness and joy.

We have touched on the topic of humility already when sharing lessons on learning, where we explored the posture of becoming "like a child" to curiously and humbly encounter the world of learning through wonder and awe.

We also included humility in our lessons on leadership, especially in terms of leading others, and that to serve others we need humble hearts.

Humility may not be the first word that comes to mind when you think about leaders, especially business leaders, like Chief Executives. I have experience working with and learning from, as well as sitting in the seat of the Chief Executive Officer. It has been my experience, which is backed up by the data when studying great businesses, that the very best leaders consistently demonstrate humility. When they look out the window they do not take credit for their success. They look for opportunities to see how their success was due to others or to fortunate external factors. They are also consistent in being willing to look in the mirror to see the real challenges and take responsibility for things that did not go well. These leaders show perseverance and determination to do what is right.

It is possible to be humbled by others, and by the poor choices we make in life, but the wisdom of humility is to intentionally choose to humble ourselves. If we build our identity around our ego and our self-importance, and if we have a sense of being entitled to get what we want, then the truth is that this pride will lead to a fall. If we aim to be humble and to be thankful for what we already have, then we face life with solid foundations and are more likely to experience contentment and joy.

I have learned that our humble hearts are more helpful and can teach us so much more than our proud minds.

It is also true that a teachable attitude is more valuable than great talent. If you are a young person wondering how to impress your boss, try being teachable and curious. My advice is to surround yourself with people from whom you can learn. You will find that you will grow in wisdom and knowledge.

One simple example of this lesson is that pride can cause us to easily judge others who appear to be struggling to navigate the challenges of life. We can intellectually compare our choices in life and judge them to be better than those made by the people around us. A humble heart is more likely to be slow to judge, understanding that it is unwise and unkind to assume that we could cope better than another person in their circumstances.

As I explained using the "windows and mirrors" analogy earlier, I have come to learn that it is not so obvious to me that if I had lived the lives of some of the people I encountered in prisons I would have done a better job than them with their start in the life.

Learning to live a life of gratitude, where we develop the intentional practice of being grateful for what we have and for those around us, lays the foundation for deep contentment and joy. This is going further than just saying thank you when someone does something nice or helpful, it is more about developing a deep appreciation for what is good in our lives.

It is not how much or how little you have that makes you happy, but it is how much you appreciate what you have that makes you happy.

In very poor and deprived communities that I have visited in South Africa, I have seen people with virtually no material wealth who are still able to be happy and appreciate what they have. It is humbling to see, because of how much I have accumulated in life.

I would argue that the more stuff you have, the more baggage you are trying to carry around. The sheer volume of material possessions is more likely to provide anxiety and envy than it is to produce joy and peace.

Neuroscience is discovering more about what brings us joy. What I find interesting is that it appears that somehow living a life of gratitude actually makes our brains more agile or flexible; better able to think new thoughts. You could say that being grateful actually makes you a little smarter. I am not surprised by these findings as this would indicate that orienting our lives to be humble and grateful is operating our minds as our original Designer intended.

I have learnt that if you intentionally direct your focus towards the people and experiences in life for which you can authentically be grateful, to see the goodness in others, then it is so much more straightforward to also show kindness. A grateful heart is a kind heart. When we recognise how much we each have to be grateful for in life, we are less inclined to compare ourselves to others. We position our hearts to also experience happiness and joy in the good in others. We learn that being kind is in itself our reward.

Sometimes kindness can express itself quite simply as being patient. A patient person has learnt humility and is willing to set aside their priorities for the other person.

Kindness is certainly not "softness." Humble and grateful hearts produce gentleness, and a focus on what is best for others, which makes us kinder and more likely to do what is good and right.

We don't "do good" as a performance to look good or to get attention. If that is our aim then that is all we will get, and we will find that it is empty.

Even if we have been entrusted with great power and influence, it is possible to have a humble approach and to hold it lightly. We can choose to use it to serve others rather than to overpower them.

A humble person, in my experience, is also quick to settle differences. They are the first to say, "I am sorry, I was wrong." They are quick to forgive others because they are fully aware of their own need for forgiveness.

This has been a lesson that I have had to learn personally, on too many occasions. I have had to humble myself to admit I was wrong on many occasions. I know that we can all find forgiveness, but it starts with forgiving others.

The sheer grace that I have experienced in life from God, and others, will always serve to humble me. It has also been one of life's great teachers.

Getting things wrong, letting others down or experiencing failure is not the end of things. For the humble, it is the arena in which we get to learn from the pain and discomfort.

As I continue to learn the lessons of humility, and the power of training to be a person of gratitude, there is a challenging question that I am wrestling with.

Am I getting more helpful and more humble as I get older?

Here is what the twenty-something learners have discovered about humility and gratitude so far:

I am learning that gratitude is not a passive process, but something that requires action. When life may seem challenging, uncomfortable or just a bit mundane, actively taking the time to look for things to be grateful for can completely transform your mindset. Put simply, finding joy in the small things is so important to happiness.

Likewise, small acts of kindness really matter to those around us.

When I look back at my teenage years, I can already see how many lessons I have learnt about humility and being grateful for small things. The truth is that when I was younger, I was not very humble. I often felt the need to show off my skills to friends and family. A decade later, I have a very different view. I am actually a lot stronger and fitter, but I have no desire to impress those around me and am more comfortable simply doing the hard work in private. I do not need to prove myself to others. A more humble path, which does not perform for the approval of others, feels like much more solid ground on which to continue my life's journey.

I am also learning that sometimes, although we may feel grateful, it is very easy to miss opportunities to clearly express our gratitude to those around us. Being intentional about expressing our gratitude towards others is so important for them, but it also serves to remind us of those we love and who love us. When we stay silent it leaves those we care for feeling underappreciated and can lead to resentment.

So remind yourself of all that is good in your life and be consistent and generous in telling others the truth about how grateful you are for them.

As twenty-something-year-old men, we think that a good life includes a good wife, a dog and a jet ski. What do you think?

Love is really beautiful when professed, but the truth is that it is only truly meaningful when it is put into practice.

Chapter 10

Lessons on Love

"But the greatest of these is love."

– 1 Corinthians 13:13

After covering some of the lessons I have learnt about what really matters, I finally come to what is the most important lesson in life. I believe this to be the greatest lesson we can all learn.

I have come to know that love is what is most important.

As you read this final chapter, you will find the underlying truths that have echoed through the lessons shared so far. You will see why I believe that all authentic and persistent pursuit of the truth will ultimately lead you to love.

I have come to learn from the Bible that there is, in fact, a "Spirit of Truth" that guides us along the path to truth. When we encounter love in its purest form, not only have we found the truth, but we also find the purest way of life. This truth leads to true freedom; freedom to love.

An authentic search for the truth starts with a pure heart. This is how we encounter the Divine. We find wholeness and unity through love, through loving one another and not through having all the right answers.

A practical example of the expression of love from the Bible is the covenant of marriage. The Bible explains that the couple leaves their parents to be joined in the covenant of marriage: a covenant that they make before God, their family and friends. They commit to love and serve each other, all the days of their lives, no matter what life brings their way.

Love is really beautiful when professed, but the truth is that it is only truly meaningful when it is put into practice.

I recently had the joy of being part of an event which will remain one of the highlights of my life: my daughter's wedding. Seeing her and my new "son" commit the rest of their lives together, in the covenant of marriage, is a memory I will always treasure. This occasion gave me the opportunity to gather my thoughts and share some of the lessons that I have learnt about love, from over three decades of marriage, with this special couple. As this chapter is about lessons on love, I thought that I would include some of what I shared at their wedding:

> "So let me close with some words of wisdom to both of you as you embark on married life together.
>
> Words really matter, so choose your words carefully.
>
> Small things matter, so keep doing the small things.
>
> Say 'thank you' to each other; gratitude is essential for ongoing happiness.
>
> Be quick to forgive each other. The weight of unforgiveness is too heavy to carry in marriage and life.

Ask for what you need; don't make your spouse guess.

Never lose the posture of a servant — serving each other is how you love each other. Love is what is most important because love covers a multitude of mistakes."

In my marriage, I have learned how love is something that grows deeper over time. It is very practical in terms of being a choice you make each day to serve your spouse. Love will always put the other person first.

One very powerful way we express our love is by giving someone our undivided attention.

One of my mentors has a very practical way of expressing this. It is the "three cups of tea" lesson. Most of us would be willing to have a cup of tea with a stranger; someone we meet for the first time. We would all also be happy to put the kettle on and have a second cup of tea when we are with friends. However, you know that you are with someone you love, someone who sees you for who you are and stays no matter what life brings, when you choose to make the third cup of tea.

Love requires the intimacy of sitting with someone to listen to their heart. Love includes sharing in the lives of those we love and, at times, it requires us to be close enough to hold each other and feel the heartbeat of the other person.

I can remember how powerful that closeness was in the precious love I experienced for my children when, as babies, they would fall asleep resting on my chest. It was love that transcended the intellectual idea of loving them. It was a deep knowing, which included all of my heart and body and soul.

I remember discussing with my wife, at the time our second child was born, that I knew that I loved my daughter with all my heart. How would it be possible to love my son as much, if my heart was already full? I discovered that the truth about true love is that is it boundless. As soon as I held him in my arms I knew that I loved him with all my heart. My love for him didn't diminish in any way how much I loved my daughter or my wife.

Love is not limited by scarcity; love is abundant.

In the years that I worked with prisons and probation, colleagues would demonstrate serving others by their actions. What I found curious was that love was not a word that anyone was comfortable speaking about in the world of prisons. It was okay to speak about treating those in our care with dignity and respect – to show our humanity. However, you would not hear someone explain the work that they did as "loving" others.

I remember a very sobering conversation with a colleague who had spent many hours earlier that week sitting on the end of the bed of a prisoner who had lost hope. The weight of their guilt and shame had become too much to bear. They were at high risk of harming themselves that night. The colleague told me that the next day the prisoner had thanked them for saving their life. The prisoner explained that it was because of what my colleague had done that got them through the night. They could now see a way forward. The colleague told me that they had not done anything apart from listening.

Sometimes that is what love requires from us – just to be there when someone has lost hope and is in real pain.

Learning to be a person of love includes learning to love ourselves, and to love who we have been created to be.

Serving others is how we love them but, if we understand love, we also need to learn how to receive it.

The example given to us from the Bible is that the Son of God received the love of the Father. If you are like me, you may find that loving yourself is not always easy. That is because I know firsthand all of my weaknesses and frailties. I know how often I let people down. I hurt the people I love. I fall short.

The truth is that any apprentice of love should look out the window to see those who are in need and serve them. We should, however, also look in the mirror and see that each one of us needs to be loved.

So, once again, we return to this humble posture that does not start with what we want but puts others first. This is the same principle we discussed in leading others. Things should be different for the apprentices of love; they serve rather than seek to be served.

My mum has already gone home to be with the Lord, but I am so grateful for her very practical example of a life lived in the service of others. My mum, from my earliest memories to the final precious time I spent with her on earth, was thinking about how she could serve others.

The strength we have is not for our status, it is for service.

As we grow in our knowledge of love, we discover that love reveals and love covers. This might seem like a contradiction but I have learnt that love is like light. It reveals the truth. If you truly love someone, then you will be willing to say things that they may not want to hear. When you say what is true, it might not be easy but it is better.

If you love someone you show your love by being more committed to their character than their comfort. Being willing to have uncomfortable conversations for someone else's good, holding up the mirror in front of them and letting them see the truth, is one of the signs that you love someone.

One example of loving others, through speaking the truth, is to set clear limits or boundaries for those with whom we have a relationship. When we know the limits or boundaries of our relationships, we then have the freedom to operate within those boundaries. Where there are no boundaries, we end up causing hurt and pain. It is not unloving to say "no." If love is only unconditional, we are extending unlimited grace but we are not framing this love within the truth. This is a recipe for chaos. It is also true that if we only impose limits and boundaries by telling the hard truth, we impose what is right, but we do not extend love and grace.

To restore order to our broken world, we all need both love and limits.

Love also "covers." Just as love requires us to be willing to say uncomfortable things, it also means being willing to have uncomfortable things said about ourselves without needing to justify, defend or blame others. Sometimes the most loving thing you can do when under a barrage of accusations and attacks, is to not respond. If defending yourself requires exposing the frailties and weaknesses of someone you love, sometimes love requires us to be silent. There is a time to be a "covering" for someone to keep them safe, rather than expose them to more pain and shame, even if this means that you take a few "blows" whilst covering them.

In senior leadership roles, especially in public service roles, it is necessary at times to provide this shield for colleagues where the consequences of exposing them would be serious. Wise and loving leaders choose to absorb these accusations and attacks to allow others to learn, grow and fail in a safe environment.

As I explained earlier, I am someone who can be tempted to try to work hard to earn acceptance. However, true love is not earned. We cannot earn God's love through obedience.

When we love, we express our love through our obedience.

We obey out of our love for someone. We don't obey to gain love.

Perhaps the most challenging test regarding loving others is to love those who intentionally mean to harm us – to love our enemies. This, according to the Bible, is the better way.

When someone is your enemy and is seeking to hurt, harm or diminish you in some way, you can choose to serve them. You can choose to love them and to pray for the best for them. To choose to do good to those who seek to harm us might be the most courageous act of freedom we can carry out.

This seems so counterintuitive and does not seem fair but, when you ponder the deep wisdom behind this approach, it is how we find true freedom in our hearts. It turns enemies into friends.

It is the worst thing that can happen to someone who is seeking to do battle with you because they don't get an adversary. They get kindness and mercy, and the Bible describes this as "heaping hot coals on their heads."

I have had the opportunity, in life and in business, to try to put this principle into practice on several occasions. It is very challenging. What I found the most difficult was how loudly my pride and ego shouted that this was not fair. Colleagues would reinforce to me that it was unfair and that I should take action, and this made doing what love requires even harder.

In my experience, this path of "loving your enemy" requires small intentional steps. It did not come naturally to me. For me, it started with praying about how I was feeling and asking for help to see beyond my pain and hurt. If you stick with this process you will find some small way to be kind to, or to be of service to, the person who has taken advantage of you or harmed you. It is then a daily and intentional choice to say and do what would be good for that person.

I must admit that I don't fully understand the full depth of this wisdom to "love your enemy." I have, however, found that when we practise it, in small but consistent ways, it sets our hearts free. Looking back, I am not carrying the baggage of bitterness and resentment. This means my load is lighter and my heart is filled with gratitude and joy.

So far I have made some progress towards learning to love and do good, to those who have harmed or intended to harm me. I still have a long way to go when it comes to loving those who harm or intend to harm my family and those I love. As I have said before, I am still a work in progress but I do aim to become a person who "loves my enemies" as a way of imitating Jesus.

Of all the lessons that I have learnt, the truth that I have discovered is that love is the better way, the much better way.

Love connects us to the divine Source. Some of the most profound insights about love can be found in the Bible, in the book of 1 Corinthians 13.

People can see through empty words and our words mean very little without love.

People appreciate generous gestures, but if they are done without love they lose their meaning.

True love is wholehearted, open-hearted and kind.

Love is willing to be patient. Love does not make a fuss. It is not easily offended and certainly does not try to enforce its way. It certainly does not keep a record of wrongs or bear a grudge.

Love is not happy when someone suffers harm. Love is not puffed up with pride but rather chooses the humble stance of a servant.

Love is resilient and can endure through the most challenging of times. What I love about love, is that it is always hopeful.

The truth about love is that it is not a feeling or an abstract concept. The truth is that love is a Person – God is love.

What we think about God may be the most important thing about us. Growing in love is therefore the highest goal we can have in life – to become a person of love.

Perhaps the most loving thing that a loving God could do is to give us the freedom to choose the way of love.

Put another way, love is the highest form of truth and it is the foundation upon which all other truths are built.

Returning to the wisdom from ancient biblical texts, the highest and greatest command is, "Love the Lord your God, with all your heart and all your mind and all your soul and all your strength." Secondly, "Love your neighbour as you love yourself" (Mark 12:30, NIVUK).

So, to become a person of love, I need to be a person who loves God. I am a person who is loved by God and a person who loves those whom God has made.

Start with the truth that God is love. He is the Source of true love. Jesus taught us that He loves us the way that God the Father loves Him (John 15:9, NIVUK). That means that God loves God.

It is such a profound truth that God loves me with the same love that God loves God.

The truest thing about me is that the One who knows me the best loves me the most.

It is due to the fact that the God of love chose to love each one of us, that we love.

Firstly, we love God. That is the first and highest purpose in life.

If we choose to be apprentices of love, then the way that we know we are following the way of love is by how we love one another. That closes the loop. We should love one another the way that the God of love loves us. Our love comes from the source of love and it overflows into loving others.

This is the never-ending journey towards truth that we all get to explore, as we humbly search for the One who is love. Like all curious learners, we start with being in awe of the one true living God. This wonder and awe is the beginning of wisdom.

In short, this better way, the way of love, never fails. Love is the greatest truth that we can come to know. Truth has a name and love has a name. That name is Jesus Christ, the Son of God.

These are the lessons on love from the twenty-something learners:

One of the best expressions of the nature of love, that I have found, is in the words recorded in the Bible (1 Corinthians 13:4–8, NIVUK):

"Love is patient and kind; love does not envy or boast; it is not arrogant or rude. It does not insist on its way; it is not irritable or resentful; it does not rejoice at wrongdoing but rejoices with the truth."

I have learned that love needs to start with learning to love yourself. We discussed in the chapter about learning to lead yourself, and the importance of knowing yourself. I am learning that love is similar. If you have not learnt to love yourself, including your flaws, then you will not be able to truly love others. I am learning that loving yourself is about accepting who you are and then believing in the person you are becoming. That could be a better son or daughter, a better sister or brother or a better husband or wife. Loving yourself means that you want what is best for you, and this is also how we love others.

I have learnt that love grows and changes over a lifetime. The love I experienced as a child centred, understandably, on my family. In adulthood, I am learning that the boundaries of love expand to include new people and new relationships, and this is making life so much richer and deeper.

I have learnt that loving someone does not mean you see them as perfect, but love means choosing to be there for that person despite their imperfections. It means working to truly understand their point of view, why they feel the way they do and what has led them to be who they are. This needs to come from a place of curiosity and understanding, and not from judgment. It often requires a lot of patience and calm communication. Certainly, for me, this continues to be a work in progress.

Although we may all have different ways of showing and feeling love, I truly believe that small acts of service are one of the most important ways of loving someone. Doing these small things can be underestimated. However, they show that you are present, are making the other person's happiness a priority and are supporting them.

Love is really about serving others.

> *True freedom is the choice to do what we ought to do. We ought to love one another.*

Conclusion

We hope that by sharing some of our life lessons, you have been inspired to think about what you have learned so far in your learning journey.

We would encourage you to take the time to let our lessons help you consider applying truth to helping you become the person you want to become. You too, can draw on the sources of truth that we continue to learn from.

We have chosen to share these lessons from our lives as our way of staying on the journey as curious learners. The writing of this book has indeed helped each one of us learn even more.

We share these lessons with humility and with gratitude for having had the opportunity to learn and to grow. Please do not misunderstand our humble and curious approach as a lack of conviction for the truths we are coming to know. We believe what we have shared and try each day to put it into practice.

Why not take the time, with the people you "do life with", to speak about what lessons you have learnt so far?

Listen carefully to lessons that they have to share and see if there is a truth that you dare to put into practice in your own life.

Hopefully, these lessons of ours will give you a glimpse through the "windows" of our lives so far. If your experience is anything like ours, don't be surprised if this gives you a "mirror" to reflect on your learning journey.

If any of these truths have been helpful to you, we would love to hear from you. Let us know what these lessons have meant to you, as we will also try to learn from your reflections.

What we have learnt about learning is to try to remain curious and in awe. Have the courage to put into practice the truth you discover.

What we have learnt about life and leadership is that, with humble hearts, there is a purpose beyond ourselves. That purpose is to serve others. Start with kindness, because it matters. We have good reason to stay hopeful and hold on to hope for those who have lost theirs.

What we have learnt about our purpose is to be good, faithful stewards of all we have, to live generously, to rest, to live within the natural rhythms of life and to remain humble and grateful.

True freedom is the choice to do what we ought to do. We ought to love one another.

So let's become the kind of people who are known for how much we love.

Remember that none of us is as smart as all of us, so we would encourage you to keep on learning.

Stay humble, kind and curious.

About the Author

Ian is a business leader whose thirty years of experience spans international private and public sector organisations, specialising in complex business services. Ian is a disruptive innovator with a track record of transforming businesses and delivering public service reform to better serve citizens, improve social justice outcomes and invest in the next generation.

Ian has held board-level roles in the private and charitable sector, and UK civil service, with accountability for multibillion-dollar programmes. In industry, Ian has led market-shaping business growth. While in the public sector, he commissioned complex operational services, such as prison and probation services across England and Wales.

Ian holds a master's degree from the University of Cambridge in Applied Criminology and Penology, as well as a Bachelor of Science in Chemistry and Applied Chemistry.

Ian has retained a long-term interest in how new technology can enable human thriving and was a contributor to a book published by the Economic Singularity Club on artificial intelligence and the future of work (Stories from 2045, ISBN 978-0-9932116-7-6, First published in 2018 by the Economic Singularity Club (ESC), page 140).

WINDOWS AND MIRRORS

Sources of Learning

Abraham Joshua Heschel

Alan Paton

Alan West

Prof. Alison Liebling FBA

Dr Andrew Huberman

Andy Stanley

Angus Buchan

Anna Theron

Ann Voskamp

Ann-Marie Conway

Anne Lamott

Archbishop Desmond Tutu

Arthur C. Brooks

Barack & Michelle Obama

Benny Lewis

Bob Goff

Bono

Dr Brené Brown

- Brother Lawrence
- Brother Yun
- Bryan Stevenson
- Cal Newport
- Calum Chace
- Carey Neuhoff
- Condoleezza Rice
- Craig Groeschel
- Dallas Willard
- Dr Danielle Hudson
- Danielle Strickland
- Dietrich Bonhoeffer
- Erwin Raphael McManus
- Eugene H. Peterson
- Francis Chan
- Frank J. Porporino
- Dr Gill Attrill OBE
- Gordon MacDonald
- Henri Nouwen
- Dr Henry Cloud
- Her Majesty Queen Elizabeth II

Jenny Porée (mum and gran)

Jewel Kilcher

Joe Rogan

John Eldredge

John Mark Comer

John Maxwell

John Ortberg

Jonathan David and Melissa Helser

Dr Jordan and Tammy Peterson

Josh Waitzkin

Ken Blanchard

Dr Larry Crabb

Marc Porée (brother and uncle)

Dr Martin Luther King Jr

Sir Martin Narey

Maya Angelou

Michael Spurr CB

N. T. Wright

Nelson Mandela

Nick Porée (dad and grandpa)

Patrick Lencioni

Paul Cowley MBE

Dr Peter Attia

Peter Scazzero

Philip M. Wheatley CB

Philip Yancey

Richard Rohr OFM

Rick Warren

Ruth Haley Barton

Dr Ruth Mann

Seth Godin

Prof. Shadd Maruna

Steffany Gretzinger

Suki Binning

Tarana Burke

Dr Timothy Keller

Sir Anthony Edward Bottoms FBA

Tracey Porée (wife)

Tyler Staton

Sir William (Bill) Thomas

Sir Winston Churchill

About PublishU

PublishU is transforming the world of publishing.

PublishU has developed a new and unique approach to publishing books, offering a three-step guided journey to becoming a globally published author!

We enable hundreds of people a year to write their book within 100-days, publish their book in 100-days and launch their book over 100-days to impact tens of thousands of people worldwide.

The journey is transformative, one author said,

"I never thought I would be able to write a book, let alone in 100 days... now I'm asking myself what else have I told myself that can't be done that actually can?'"

To find out more visit
www.PublishU.com

Printed in Great Britain
by Amazon